Sidney Lanier,
Henry Timrod,
and
Paul Hamilton Hayne

a reference guide

A
Reference
Publication
in
Literature

Joseph Katz
Editor

Sidney Lanier,
Henry Timrod,
and
Paul Hamilton Hayne

a reference guide

JACK DE BELLIS

G.K.HALL &CO.

70 LINCOLN STREET, BOSTON, MASS.

Library of Congress Cataloging in Publication Data
De Bellis, Jack.
    Sidney Lanier, Henry Timrod, and Paul Hamilton Hayne.

    (Reference publications in literature)
    Includes indexes.
    1. American poetry — 19th century — History and criticism —
Bibliography.   2. American poetry — Southern States —
History and criticism — Bibliography.   3. Lanier, Sidney,
1842–1881 — Bibliography.   4. Timrod, Henry, 1828–1867 —
Bibliography.   5. Hayne, Paul Hamilton, 1830–1886 —
Bibliography.   I. Title.   II. Series.
Z1227.D4   [PS316]   016.811'.4'09   77-17203
ISBN 0-8161-7967-0

This publication is printed on permanent/durable acid-free paper
MANUFACTURED IN THE UNITED STATES OF AMERICA

Contents

Sidney Lanier

Introduction

Unlike other important nineteenth-century Southern poets, Sidney Lanier was a public figure at the end of his life. As a musician he had risen to notice while playing in orchestras and salons in Baltimore and New York. His own compositions attracted attention, and he was called "the Wagner of American music." As a poet, he gained prominence when Bayard Taylor gave him the opportunity to write the poem which Dudley Buck set to music as the "Centennial Cantata" in 1876. The subsequent notoriety brought Lanier a new conviction that he would become a great poet. His Poems appeared in 1877. In 1880 he published a controversial study of the relationship between music and poetry, The Science of English Verse. At the same time he lectured at Johns Hopkins University on Shakespeare and the development of the novel, using the innovative psychological approach. A conspicuous Southern gentleman in the North, with a transcendental reverence for nature, Lanier was a significant spokesman for national unity and social progress in the Reconstruction South. Projecting volumes of verse which would delineate the psychological complexity of the soul's journey, publishing guide books and pot boilers to morally rearm the Gilded Age, asserting in his prose frequently the etherealization of all aspects of the nineteenth century as well as a synthetic view of religion and science, Lanier was a figure of interest.

But this energetic activity occurred at a time of great hardship, and the early Lanier criticism was strongly influenced by the pathos of his poverty and lingering death from tuberculosis. He presented not only the conventional symbol of the poet nipped in the bud, but a prime example of Southern knighthood, a specimen of "the chivalry" not capable of ridicule. He effectively established a bulwark against the North's condescension to Southern literature. This came to be the official Southern view of Lanier, but with the development of the "Southern Renaissance" after 1925 a different view emerged.

By 1900 interest in synthesis between the arts had begun to decline, and the rise of Imagism and development of "free verse" had examined rather thoroughly the relations of music to poetic rhythm. Lanier's theory of a "science" of English verse thus came under intense scrutiny. Critics would continue to claim that his marriage of music and poetry was Lanier's "genius" but they would also indicate

3

that it contributed to obscurity and strain, thwarting his spontaneity and causing him to write from a "formula." But since Lanier had spoken of these matters with the prestige of a Johns Hopkins lectern and a Peabody Orchestra chair, criticism of his aesthetics continued to be unsettled. It remains the pre-eminent concern of Lanier critics.

Meanwhile, other critics had been concerned with the ethical and social content of his work, particularly since Lanier thereby offered a buffer to the encroachments of science on religion and Naturalism on the arts. Dudley Miles (1918.B3) saw Lanier's "moral earnestness" as making the union of North and South possible. Some felt that Lanier's social consciousness, revealed in the poetry of the early 1870's, helped to raise a protest against the excesses of the "Tragic Era." Edwin Mims (1926.B4) suggested that Lanier provided a vision of a New South, and Aubrey Starke in his Lanier biography (1933.A1) intensified this argument. Vernon Parrington (1930.B4) had seen Lanier as rejecting the genteel tradition and middle class alike. Depending on their view of Lanier's didactic Christian attitudes, such critics took heart from his criticism of "art for art's sake" and Walt Whitman.

The most important controversy in Lanier criticism, apart from his aesthetic theories, concerned his importance to modern America. Aubrey Starke's biography of Lanier asserted that Lanier helped to create not only the New South but also the Southern Renaissance. Reviews by members of that movement (Robert Penn Warren, Allen Tate and John Crowe Ransom) and Starke's replies revealed the distance that modern writers felt from Lanier's techniques as well as his ideas. As New Critics they found his poetry lacking in paradox, wit, irony, consistency in metaphor and symbolism and clarity of design. As members of the Fugitive-Agrarian movement, they rejected Starke's attempt to make a Southern hero of one who had apparently championed the materialism and progressivism he professed to despise. Shackford (1940.B9, B10, B11) and De Bellis (1972.A1) treated these charges as mistaken readings of Lanier and faulty logic. Nevertheless, the view of Ransom, Warren and Tate has persisted.

Various attempts to place Lanier in the history of ideas substantiated his historical importance. While Philip Graham's Lanier's Thought in Relation to that of his Age (1927.A1) was the first extensive work of this kind, the edition of Lanier's poetry, prose and letters, under the general editorship of Charles R. Anderson (1945.B1, B2) was the first systematic, scholarly analysis of Lanier's sources and influences. De Bellis's Sidney Lanier and the Morality of Feeling (1964.A1) placed him in the moral sentiments tradition, while Elmer Havens's Sidney Lanier's Concept and Use of Nature (1965.A1) examined his work in the light of evolution and ancillary theories.

Although Anderson's Centennial Edition of the Works of Sidney Lanier (1945.B1, B2) stimulated study of Lanier's place in the history of ideas and provoked some textual criticism, as well as additions to Lanier's canon and letters, prevailing critical opinion since 1945 has been unfavorable. Few analyses of his work have appeared and the tone of the established critics is dismissive. Edd Winfield Parks in 1968 (A2) held the same view he maintained in 1936 (B12), that Lanier was never able to fuse his philosophical interests to his aesthetic technique; consequently, he remained didactic, sentimental and vague. Roy Harvey Pearce (1961.A1) considered Lanier mistaken about his media and his audience, thus unable to follow the directions of either Whitman or Dickinson.

Lanier's reasons for his interest in nature, often thought to be his primary successful concern, have been challenged. Parrington (1930.B4) and Williams (1931.B9) suggested that Lanier's view of nature was pagan, and Leon Howard (1960.B1) pronounced nature an avenue of escape. Edmund Wilson in 1962 (B4) as in 1946 (B11) guessed that for Lanier, nature was an ideal replacing the Lost Cause. Although Lanier's handling of nature had been accepted at the beginning of the twentieth century as a way of sacrificing lucidity for spiritual force, Leary (1947.B8) saw Lanier's obscurity as typical of the Southern overvaluation of feeling. Ross (1961.B2) found "The Marshes of Glynn" simply a failure because of its obscurity, and despite Harry Warfel's systematic positive exploration of the poem (1965.B8), Hyatt Waggoner has ridiculed it for its vague and confused treatment of nature (1968.B8).

Other claims often made previously for Lanier have also received strictures. His nationalism has been criticized of course by Ransom, Tate and Warren, but also by Wilson (1962.B4) and England (1964.B3) who see Lanier as a "son of the South." Even Lanier's musical compositions have been described by Edwards as unoriginal (1968.B4).

Wilson's reiteration of an earlier idea that Lanier was among America's truest men of letters has thus been upheld only in part. His connections between music and poetry, however, have continued to provoke critical argument. Lenhart (1956.B4) and Brown (1948.B1, 1965.B3) have not found Lanier's handling of music in his poetry or as a general theory very successful, although Hendren (1959.B3) has staunchly defended Lanier's <u>Science of English Verse</u> against them, as well as against Paull Baum's comments in his introduction to his edition of the work for <u>The Centennial Edition</u>. Although William Carlos Williams was at first quite impressed by Lanier's study (1953.B4) he later changed his mind (1959.B7). But another important poet, Karl Shapiro, pronounced Lanier's study "justly famous" (1948.B7). Other commentators like De Bellis (1972.A1) have not sought to evaluate the significance of the theory, but simply indicate that it was a logical development for a poet concerned with amplifying his technical resources in order to make his moral attitudes more emphatic.

Lanier's present position is thus both admirable and unhappy. A few dedicated scholars have made Lanier's literary record the envy of all other American writers. His biography is definitive. His poetry and major prose have been set in a scholarly record of copious fact. His poetry has a concordance. His personal epistolary life

is virtually completely visible. He has received an authoritative
bibliography (Graham and Thies, 1945) without which this reference
guide could not have been written. His sources have been described,
and several attempts have been made to place him in the history of
ideas. Yet these things have not stimulated the critical interest
that might have been expected. Instead, there is a growing feeling
that Lanier has received enough attention to substantiate the belief
that he is a minor figure who never achieved full promise and whose
art was never fully unified or defined. My own study of Lanier
(1972.A1) sought to counter this feeling by stressing the essential
unification of Lanier's life and work.

It has been my intention in this reference guide to include everything written about Lanier which might be of worth to the student and
specialist. With a half-dozen exceptions, every item in this guide
contains an annotation which varies in length according to the value
of the itemized work. In all cases the annotation indicates the area
of interest and the general value of the item. No attempt has been
made to make a complete record of writings about Lanier, since most
newspaper articles and most graduate theses have not been listed.
Also, many items of the nineteenth century have been excluded. However, virtually everything written on Lanier since 1945 has been
itemized and annotated. The index lists authors, titles, and subjects, with Lanier's own work included within the general index,
rather than separated under the poet's name.

Writings about
Sidney Lanier, 1868–1976

1868 A BOOKS - NONE

1868 B SHORTER WRITINGS

   1   ANON. Review of <u>Tiger-Lilies</u>. <u>Atlantic</u>, XXI (March), 382.
         Finds the novel too derivative but predicts Lanier
would do better considering the nobility of Southern life
and the wealth of Northern villains available.

1869 A BOOKS - NONE

1869 B SHORTER WRITINGS

   1   DAVIDSON, JAMES WOOD. <u>Living Writers of the South</u>. New York:
         Carleton, pp. 321–324.
            <u>Tiger-Lilies</u> is "a spirited story of Southern life."
[Due to a printer's error the plate of p. 320 of Davidson's
book was mistakenly placed, causing several pages of this
essay to be lost.]

1875 A BOOKS - NONE

1875 B SHORTER WRITINGS

   1   ANON. Comments on "The Symphony." <u>Nation</u>, XX (27 May), 362.
         Selected by the <u>Nation</u> as the second most noticeable
poem in June magazines because it is "fluent, fanciful and
sweet, not over-sensible," and worth reading for its
"fancy," despite being "hurt by mannerisms both of expression and sentiment."

   2   ANON. Comments on <u>Florida</u>. <u>Nation</u>, XXI (28 October), 277.
         Comments on sketches of Florida appearing in <u>Lippincott's</u>
<u>Magazine</u> by Lanier. Finds his style has submitted to the
"rhetorical-poetical foible" of "seeing God in everything."

1876

1876 A BOOKS – NONE

1876 B SHORTER WRITINGS

1   ANON. Review of <u>Florida</u>. <u>Nation</u>, XXII (27 January), 63.
        Finds Lanier's guidebook to Florida, "the best of its
     kind."

2   ANON. Comments on publication of "The Centennial Cantata."
        <u>Nation</u>, XXII (13 April), 247.
           Attacks Lanier's poem because it "reads like a communi-
     cation from the spirit of Nat Lee, rendered through a Bed-
     lamite medium," and accuses the poem of "emancipation from
     the ordinary laws of sense and sound, melody and prosody."

3   ANON. Notes on Lanier's Reactions to the <u>Nation</u>'s Criticism
        of "The Centennial Cantata." <u>Nation</u>, XXII (25 May), 336.
           Extracts Lanier's letter to the New York <u>Tribune</u> in which
     he accused the <u>Nation</u> of being unfair in reviewing his work
     as a poem, rather than as a lyric to be sung. <u>Nation</u> re-
     plies that "Lanier's poetic sensibility and serious purpose
     cannot make up for the lack of clear expression in his
     writing."

4   ANON. Review of <u>Poems</u>. <u>New York Times</u>, XXVI (2 December), 3.
           Examines "The Symphony" and "Corn" carefully, concluding
     that "Corn" is superior because it is deeply attached to
     Southern life and is particularly meritorious in neither
     supporting nor condemning the "South's habit of borrowing
     and repudiating" depicted in the poem. Admires "The Sym-
     phony" for its wedding of poetry and music and declares
     that its criticism of the evils of commercialism is rooted
     in the Southern temper. Asserts that the other poems are
     not the equal of "Corn" and "The Symphony" because they are
     either too cold or show that Lanier "read Swinburne too
     much."

5   [APTHORP, W. F.]. Review of "The Centennial Cantata."
        <u>Atlantic</u>, XXXVIII (July), 122–124.
           Suggests that Lanier's poem could have been made into a
     better song by a composer like Wagner.

1877 A BOOKS - NONE

1877 B SHORTER WRITINGS

1   ANON. Review of Lanier's Poems. Nation, XXIV (4 January),
     16.
         Argues that while Lanier shows a genuine feeling for
     nature in "Corn," he lacks simplicity and writes in a "con-
     vulsive" mode.

2   ANON. Review of Lanier's Poems. Harper's, LIV (March),
     617-618.
         Finds the poems reveal "genuine poetic genius."

3   LANIER, J. F. D. Sketch of the Life of J. F. D. Lanier.
     Place of publication and publisher not given.
         J. F. D. Lanier recounts the story of his financial and
     political success in New York for the private edification
     of the Lanier family. Sidney Lanier read this and sent him
     a "Geneology" of the Lanier family, printed at the end of
     the Sketch.

1879 A BOOKS - NONE

1879 B SHORTER WRITINGS

1   ANON. "A Masque of Transatlantic Poets." Spectator, LII
     (22 February), 247-248.
         Reviews A Masque of Poets, to which Lanier contributed
     "The Marshes of Glynn," and finds the marsh poem "one of
     the few poems which show signs of power." Cautions Lanier
     to keep his adjectives "quiet."

2   ANON. Review of The Boy's Froissart. Nation, XXIX
     (4 December), 392.
         Praises Lanier for his excellent introduction, explain-
     ing to boys what true chivalry means to the nineteenth
     century. Credits Lanier with good judgment in his organi-
     zation of the stories.

1880 A BOOKS - NONE

1880 B SHORTER WRITINGS

1   ANON. Review of The Boy's Froissart. Appleton's Journal,
     VIII (January), 96.

1880

Praises Lanier for eliminating the drier descriptive passages and tedious dialogue, while retaining all the "spirit, and fire, and romance" of the original.

2   ANON. Review of The Boy's Froissart. Atlantic, XLV (January), 130.
Observes that the Southern fondness for jousts has been turned to useful account with this book. Welcomes this book "most heartily" for its skillful condensing.

3   ANON. Review of The Boy's Froissart. Harper's, LX (February), 474.
Admires the book for its "unusual excellence" in arranging the disconnected stories.

4   ANON. "The Science of Poetry." New York Times, XXIX (18 June), 3.
Argues that despite Lanier's superior taste and judgment in music and poetry he is basically wrong in thinking there is a "science" of verse since poetry, unlike music, is not grounded in the physics of sounds. Poetry cannot be created by rules.

5   ANON. Review of The Science of English Verse. New Englander, XXXIX (July), 566–567.
Credits Lanier with "nice discriminations," though his style is too technical.

6   ANON. "Lanier's Science of English Verse." Scribner's, XX (July), 473–474.
Predicts that this "most important and most original work of versification" will meet with hostility and ridicule. Claims it is most original, "and most undoubtedly right," in its theory of rhythm.

7   ANON. "Lanier's Science of English Verse." Literary World, XI (3 July), 227.
Perceives "suggestive truth" in the book, but also detects many errors and fears it will only increase the number of poet-tasters.

8   ANON. Review of "The New South." Nation, XXXI (23 September), 223.
Finds a "palatable husk of philosophy and history" injected into this economics study.

9   ANON. Review of The Science of English Verse. Harper's, LXI (October), 796–797.

10

Describes the book as a "valuable, historical outline...
[with] thorough technical knowledge...[and] keen analogies"
useful to amateur and professional alike.

10   ANON. "Lanier's Science of English Verse." Nation, XXXI
      (28 October), 310–311.
          Reviews the book carefully and discovers these faults:
      not knowing musical notation is a decided handicap; it is
      untrue that a musician can tell the difference between
      pitches precisely; and, most important, the mass of English
      poetry is not in "3/8 time" as Lanier claims, but in 2/4
      rhythm. Yet the work shows extensive reading and refined
      taste in poetry and music.

11   ANON. Review of The Boy's King Arthur. Scribner's, XXI
      (December), 322–323.
          Lauds Lanier for a tender reverence for the integrity of
      the text and his sensitivity for condensation.

12   ANON. Review of The Boy's King Arthur. Literary World, XI
      (4 December), 441.
          Asserts that boys will learn character-building without
      fail from stories of knightly action.

13   BROWNE, FRANCIS F. "The Mechanism of Poetry." Dial, I
      (July), 55–58.
          Observes that Lanier pushed farther than any of his
      predecessors in attempting to determine laws by which form
      produces poetic effects. Concludes that Lanier established
      a sound foundation for more important generalizations.

1881 A BOOKS - NONE

1881 B SHORTER WRITINGS

1   ANON. Review of The Boy's King Arthur. Atlantic, XLVII
     (January), 122–123.
         Lauds Lanier for his "excellent judgment in editing,"
     grouping the tales around specific knights and carefully
     dropping out of sight "all grossness."

2   ANON. Review of The Boy's King Arthur. Academy, XXX
     (1 January), 7.
         Warmly recommends the book.

3   ANON. Review of The Science of English Verse. Critic, I
     (15 January), 14.
         Briefly notices the publication of the book.

1881

4 ANON. Obituary. <u>Nation</u>, XXXIII (15 September), 216.
  Finds Lanier's poetry was "eminently thoughtful and
  studied" to the neglect of lyricism and humor. Predicts
  that his meager output will destine him to be classed with
  the magazine poets who were his inferiors.

5 ANON. "Sidney Lanier." <u>Harper's Weekly</u>, XXV (24 September),
  653.
  Maintains that a man of real genius has been lost, along
  with his great promise.

6 ANON. Obituary. <u>Dial</u>, II (November), 154.
  Finds Lanier's demise cut short the life of "one of the
  most promising of our younger men of letters."

7 ANON. Obituary. <u>Nation</u>, XXXIII (17 November), 394.
  Recounts how at the October 22 Commemoration Meeting at
  Johns Hopkins University, Lanier was regarded as a man of
  "rarest spirit" on the verge of "national recognition."

8 ANON. Review of <u>The Boy's Mabinogion</u>. <u>Dial</u>, II (December),
  182–183.
  Suggests that Lanier succeeded in his attempt to "entice
  his fellow man to profit by the fruits of his zealous and
  generous labor."

9 ANON. Review of <u>The Boy's Mabinogion</u>. <u>Literary World</u>, XII
  (3 December), 449.
  Commends this "excellent holiday book" for being well
  done, with a useful pronunciation guide.

10 STEDMAN, EDMUND C. "The Late Sidney Lanier." <u>Critic</u>, I
  (5 November), 298.
  A letter read by Stedman as a tribute given on October
  22. Reprinted 1911.B5.

11 WILLARD, FRANCES E. "Notes of Southern Literary Men and
  Women." <u>Independent</u>, XXXIII (1 September), 3–4.
  Recounts hearing Lanier lecture at Johns Hopkins, describing him as "more than a raconteur...different from a
  bibliophile." Lanier spoke kindly of her work.

1882 A BOOKS - NONE

1882 B SHORTER WRITINGS

1 ANON. Review of <u>The Boy's Percy</u>. <u>Independent</u>, XXXIV
  (23 November), 10.

Observes that literature was the greatest expression of man to Lanier, so boy's books have the highest aims.

2   ANON. Review of The Boy's Percy. Nation, XXXV (30 November), 468.
    Avers that Lanier's poetic sense could be trusted "to choose what is good as literature." Consequently, he excised everything "unclean."

1883 A BOOKS - NONE

1883 B SHORTER WRITINGS

1   ANON. Review of The Boy's Percy. Harper's, LXVI (January), 316.
    Finds the selections "in every way admirable."

2   ANON. Review of The Boy's Percy. Academy, XXIII (7 April), 237-238.
    Maintains that this boy's book surpasses in interest all of Lanier's previous efforts for boys.

3   ANON. "Sidney Lanier on the English Novel." Critic, III (19 May), 228-229.
    Suggests that Lanier's strained quotes and exaggerations which led to placing George Eliot at the head of English novelists might have resulted from his chivalry--as might his attack on Walt Whitman. Yet these provincial appraisals are "suggestive of thought."

4   ANON. Review of The English Novel. Dial, IV (June), 40-41.
    Discovers suggestions of Taine's critical mind in Lanier's philosophical insight into fiction. Surmises that although the essays are unfinished, they are more effective that way.

5   ANON. "Sidney Lanier's Lectures." Literary World (Boston), XIV (30 June), 204-205.
    Criticizes Lanier for not revising his lectures, thus creating many digressions and committing too much of the book to George Eliot. Maintains The English Novel is not essentially a study of the novel's development, but rather is a loosely gathered collection of ideas, some of which are rich in noble attitudes in linking ancient writers to the moderns.

6   ANON. Review of The English Novel. Nation, XXXVII (12 July), 38.

1883

Calls this study "an apotheosis of George Eliot," but
cites its major weakness as incomplete substantiation of
its argument--that the evolution of music, fiction, science
and personality occurred at the same time and reached their
zenith in George Eliot's works. The book seems thus to be
a case of special pleading, with Lanier a victim of his in-
fatuation. Careful revision might have kept him for exalt-
ing fiction over drama and Eliot over Shakespeare.

7 ANON. Review of The English Novel. Independent, XXXV
   (6 September), 12.
      Recognizes that Lanier's criticism is of the noblest,
   most inspiring sort, but resents the omission of any comment
   on Emerson as a poet.

8 ANON. Review of The English Novel. Harper's, LXVII
   (October), 798-799.
      Discovers that despite the book's inequalities, it is
   the best recent fiction criticism because of great subtlety
   in which it shows how music, personality, and the novel all
   became important to modern man simultaneously.

1884 A BOOKS - NONE

1884 B SHORTER WRITINGS

1 ANON. Review of Lanier's Poems. Nation, XXXIX (18 December),
   528.
      Assumes that this first "truly Southern poet" will be
   raised to a higher position by this edition of his collected
   poems, since his later poems were superior to those of his
   1877 volume. In fact, "Sunrise" showed he was beyond Whitman in "affluence, breadth, handling," though Lanier was
   "suffused with more light."

2 PENN, ARTHUR. "Sidney Lanier on the English Novel." Century
   Magazine (New York), XXVII (April), 957-958.
      Contends that all future critics of the novel must take
   The English Novel into account.

3 STODDARD, F. H. "The Ideal in Literature." New Englander,
   XLIII (January), 97-104.
      Suggests that these "almost perfect" lectures fail in
   subtle discriminations between the moral and the didactic.
   Takes "intensest delight" in the work's "desultoryness."

4 THAYER, WILLIAM. "Sidney Lanier and His Poetry."
   <u>Independent</u>, XXXVI (12 June), 742–743.
      Discovers the "Western Spirit" of freedom in every line
   of Lanier's, and names his talent "intellectual rather than
   emotional, reflective, rather than passionate."

5 ____. "Lanier's Poems." <u>Independent</u>, XXXVI (18 December),
   1609.
      Observes that Lanier, still ignored by critics, was mis-
   treated while alive by them. Thinks this inexplicable since
   love was the feature of his soul as music was of his poetry.
   Provides an overview of his main poems, considering them
   ("Sunrise," "The Bee" and "Clover") to be "artist's situations."

6 ____. "Sidney Lanier's Poems." <u>American</u>, IX (20 December),
   167–168.
      Compares Lanier with Keats, finding Lanier to be broader
   and saner, with greater purity and less morbidity, and with
   better music.

7 WARD, WILLIAM HAYES. "Memorial," in <u>The Poems of Sidney
   Lanier</u>. Edited by Mary Day Lanier. New York: Scribner's,
   pp. xi–xli.
      Focuses on the pathos of Lanier's life, as well as the
   pursuit of his genius. Notes his mind was "as truly philo-
   sophically and scientifically accurate, as it was poetically
   sensuous and imaginative." So his scientific quest into
   the laws of verse led to deeper regard for the "holiness of
   beauty." Reprinted in 1884.B8 and other editions of
   Lanier's poems in 1891, 1894, 1896, 1897, 1899, 1900, 1903,
   1904, 1906, 1908, 1910, 1912, 1913, and 1929.

8 ____. "Sidney Lanier, Poet." <u>Century Magazine</u>, XXVII
   (April), 816–21.
      Reprint of 1884.B7.

1885 A BOOKS - NONE

1885 B SHORTER WRITINGS

1 ANON. "Poems of Sidney Lanier." <u>Literary News</u>, VI
   (January), 9–10.
      Lauds Lanier for his depth of feeling, earnestness of
   expression, and nobility of aim. Though he saw poetry
   served sacred ends because he tried to "express too much,"
   his life was greater than his poems.

1885

2 ANON. Review of Lanier's <u>Poems</u>. <u>Critic</u>, III (3 January), 3-4.
   Cites Ward for his "beautiful and touching" "Memorial," and the poems for their "vivid and controlled imagination" unknown twenty years before.

3 ANON. Review of Lanier's <u>Poems</u>. <u>Atlantic</u>, LV (February), 288.
   Finds Lanier a "true musician" who might have given "noble melodies" once he mastered his instrument.

4 ANON. "Sidney Lanier's Poems." <u>Literary World</u>, XVI (February), 40-41.
   Holds that although Lanier was born with a poetic temperament, he never found the power of song.

5 ANON. Review of Lanier's <u>Poems</u>. <u>Lippincott's Magazine</u>, XXXV (May), 525-526.
   Maintains that admiration for Lanier's poems finally rests on response to his noble, charming personality, which, like Keats's, was best displayed in his poems about nature.

6 BROWNE, F. F. Review of Lanier's <u>Poems</u>. <u>Dial</u>, V (January), 244-246.
   Guesses these poems were only "testing of poetic notes whose full harmony he never sounded."

7 CHAMBERLAIN, D. H. "The Poems of Sidney Lanier." <u>New Englander</u>, LXIV (March), 227-238.
   Asserts that Ward overpraised Lanier, since his poetry was fragmentary, hindered and "almost rudimentary," and only his marsh poems were really rhythmic. Examines Lanier's primary poems by types--elegy, ballad, etc. Concludes that the dialect poems "disfigure" his serious work, but that "praise can hardly be excessive" for "The Psalm of the West."

8 GATES, MERRILL E. "Sidney Lanier's Moral Earnestness." <u>Critic</u>, VI (9 May), 227.
   Asserts that Lanier's indication that moral purpose was the only worthy inspiration of the artist would have made him "a power" had he written no poetry. <u>See</u> 1888.A2.

9 STEDMAN, EDMUND C. <u>Poets of America</u>. Boston: Houghton Mifflin, pp. 449-51.
   Explains Lanier's difficulties by the trait "which made his genius unique"--his musical compulsion. Yet this created "the strained effect of several ambitious failures."

10   WARD, WILLIAM HAYES. "Memorial," in <u>The Poems of Sidney</u>
        <u>Lanier</u>. Edited by Mary Day Lanier. New York: Scribner's,
        pp. xi–xli.
            Reprint of 1884.B6.

<u>1886 A BOOKS – NONE</u>

<u>1886 B SHORTER WRITINGS</u>

1   HAYNE, PAUL HAMILTON. "A Poet's Letters to a Friend."
        <u>Critic</u> (New York), VIII (13 February), 77–78.
            Hayne's notes reveal his early realization that Lanier's
        early style was a compound of literary loves and his per-
        sonal quaintness. In these letters 1869–1871 Lanier ex-
        plains that his "sympathies" are stronger than his will,
        notes that the artist should not despise praise, and remarks
        that he feels that Hayne's view of poetry is, like his own,
        high and humble. Confides that he read a Hayne poem to
        friends, among whom was Jefferson Davis, and includes de-
        tailed, supportive criticism of Hayne's "Fire Pictures."
        Hayne indicates that some of the letters are like prose-
        poems with "exquisite delicacy of fancy." Reprinted:
        1899.B8.

2   _____. "A Poet's Letters to a Friend." <u>Critic</u> (New York),
        VIII (20 February), 89–90.
            Lanier describes in his letters 1871–1880 to Paul Hamil-
        ton Hayne the "dramatic <u>verve</u>" discoverable in Hayne's poem
        "The Macrobian Bow"; insists that his essential artistic
        ability is musical, not poetical; praises the "heavenly
        fires" of Hayne's "Cloud-Star"; delineates his success as
        flutist with the Peabody Orchestra; and limns his poverty
        and illness. Hayne's small note characterizes the tone of
        the letters as alternating between "feverish exaltation"
        and "profound despondency." Reprinted: 1899.B8.

3   WILKINSON, WILLIAM CLEAVER. "One More Homage to Sidney
        Lanier." <u>Independent</u>, XXXVIII (7 October), 1261.
            Examines several poems to conclude that Lanier was "too
        fine and high to be properly called great." His intensity
        led to defects of mannerism and quaintness.

1887

1887 A BOOKS

1   GATES, MERRILL E. <u>Sidney Lanier--a Paper</u>. New Brunswick,
New Jersey: privately printed, 32pp.
Reprint of 1887.B2. <u>See</u> 1888.B2.

1887 B SHORTER WRITINGS

1   COLEMAN, CHARLES W. "The Recent Movement in Southern
Literature." <u>Harper's</u>, LXXIV (May), 837–855.
    Provides a context for understanding Lanier's contribu-
tion to post-Civil War fiction.

2   GATES, MERRILL E. "Sidney Lanier." <u>Presbyterian Review</u>, VIII
(October), 669–701.
    Presents a biographical sketch in order to show how
Lanier blended "loyalty to the loftiest moral truth" and
"the richest gifts of poetic imagination and utterance."
Reprinted: 1887.A1. <u>See</u> 1888.B2.

3   HANKINS, VIRGINIA. "Some Memories of Lanier." <u>Southern
Bivouac</u>, II (May), 760–761.
    Recalling his exploits during the War of Secession and
his dedication to the literary life, predicts his biographer
will record the "steadfastness" of the man whose life was a
"satisfying symphony."

4   HIGGINSON, THOMAS WENTWORTH. "Sidney Lanier." <u>Chautauquan</u>,
VII (April), 416–418.
    Reviewing Lanier's life and work, finds him a "master-
singer" whose poetry is superior to Paul Hamilton Hayne's
and who will long be known as the "Sir Galahad of American
poets." Reprinted: 1899.B9.

1888 A BOOKS

1   BOYKIN, LAURETTE NISBET. <u>Home Life of Sidney Lanier</u>.
Atlanta, Georgia: J. P. Harrison, 12pp.
    Lanier's homelife is typified by love of God and family.

2   GILMAN, DANIEL C. <u>The Forty-Sixth Birthday of Sidney Lanier</u>.
Baltimore, Maryland: The Johns Hopkins University Press,
56pp.
    Contents: an introduction by Gilman who summarizes let-
ters from James Russell Lowell and E. C. Stedman; Merrill E.
Gates' "On the Ethical Influence of Lanier" which finds

Lanier's work throbbing "with all-embracing love for his
fellow-men, for all that has life, and for the entire uni-
verse of order and beauty"; Albert H. Tolman's "Lanier's
Science of English Verse," which stresses the error of considering all verse to be lyric; and a bibliography by R. E.
Burton. See 1885.B8 and 1888.B5.

3   WEST, CHARLES N. <u>A Brief Sketch of the Life and Writings of
      Sidney Lanier</u>. Savannah, Georgia: Townsend, 25pp.
           Sketches Lanier's life, stressing his national pride and
      hope for the future. Considers the lectures on literature,
      "the richest coinage of Lanier's mind."

<u>1888 B SHORTER WRITINGS</u>

1   ANON. Review of tributes to Lanier at the "Forty-Sixth
      Birthday." <u>Nation</u>, XLVI (9 February), 118-119.
           Recounts the tributes to Lanier, noting that "he has
      never been a popular poet--perhaps never will be." See
      1888.A2.

2   ANON. Review of tributes to Lanier at the "Forty-Sixth
      Birthday." <u>Critic</u>, XII (5 May), 224.
           Extracts letters received at the Lanier Memorial festiv-
      ities, among them recounting how Lowell recalled Lanier's
      "shining presence" and how Stedman mourned that death
      halted Lanier's "ultimate design." See 1888.A2.

3   ANON. "The Lanier Memorial." <u>Critic</u>, XII (19 May), 245.
           Replies to Gates's view of Lanier, declaring he lacked
      spontaneity and was inferior to Poe. See 1887.A1, 1887.B2.

4   BUCKHAM, JAMES. "In Honor of Lanier." <u>Literary World</u>, XIX
      (18 February), 56-57.
           Describes the tributes to Lanier at the "Forty-Sixth
      Birthday," noting that two Johns Hopkins' poets offered
      poems to Lanier. Remarks he would have been in the front
      rank of American poets had he lived, because of his "wonder-
      fully sweet and beautiful lyrics."

5   B[URTON], R[ICHARD] E. "A Lanier Memorial." <u>Critic</u>, XII
      (11 February), 63-64.
           Describes every event in the memorial tributes at Johns
      Hopkins, "The Forty-Sixth Birthday of Sidney Lanier." Enu-
      merates the reading of letters and poems, the performance
      of music (some songs fashioned from Lanier poems), and the
      bust of Lanier by Ephraim Keyser. Reprinted in 1888.A2.

1888

6   GOSSE, EDMUND. "Has America Produced a Poet?" <u>Forum</u>, VI
(October), 176–186.
Finds that tortured fancy and vague rhetoric typified
Lanier's poetry. Reprinted: 1893.B2.

7   HIGGINSON, THOMAS WENTWORTH. "The Victory of the Weak," in
<u>Women and Men</u>. New York: Harper Brothers, pp. 296–300.
Lanier's rejection of "survival of the fittest" philos-
ophies in <u>The English Novel</u> is admired by Higginson.

8   MORRIS, HARRISON S. "The Poetry of Sidney Lanier." <u>American
Weekly</u> (Philadelphia), XV (18 February), 284–285.
Argues that Lanier not only makes us think but "makes us
<u>be</u>." Finds he recorded "the beauty which is truth,"
despite the "mechanisms" of his final poems.

9   RICHARDSON, CHARLES F. <u>American Literature: 1607–1885</u>.
Vol. II. New York: Putnam's, pp. 231–232.
Remarks that no one can fail to recognize in Lanier's
poetry the "time-spirit, the land-song and the true poetic
touch," though his verse theories were fatal to his spontaneity. Notes that Timrod and Hayne were not hindered
thus.

10 SCOTT, W. J. "Life and Genius of Sidney Lanier." <u>Quarterly
Review of Methodist Episcopal Church, South</u> (Nashville,
Tennessee), V (October), 157–171.
The editor of <u>Scott's Magazine</u> recalls meeting Lanier in
1867 in Alabama, and attests to the "lofty idealism" of the
early work of Lanier.

11 WARD, WILLIAM HAYES. "Memorial," in <u>The Poems of Sidney
Lanier</u>. Edited by Mary Day Lanier. New York: Scribner's,
pp. xi–xli.
Reprint of 1884.B7.

1889 A BOOKS – NONE

1889 B SHORTER WRITINGS

1   ANON. "Sidney Lanier," in <u>Biographical Souvenir of Georgia
and Florida</u>. Chicago: F. A. Battey, pp. 502–503.
Brief biographical sketch of Lanier.

2   ANON. "Clifford Lanier," in <u>Biographical Souvenir of Georgia
and Florida</u>. Chicago: F. A. Battey, pp. 501–502.
Brief biographical sketch of Sidney Lanier's brother.

1890 A BOOKS - NONE

1890 B SHORTER WRITINGS

1   ANON. "Sidney Lanier." Spectator (London), LXV
    (6 December), 828–829.
        Finds Lanier the most original poet in England or America
    of the past thirty years with "no easily assignable limit
    to [his] genius."

2   HILL, W. B. "Sidney Lanier." Atlanta Constitution (Atlanta,
    Georgia), (19 October), p. 11.
        Offers a description of the events at the unveiling of a
    Keyser bust of Lanier in Macon. Provides extracts from let-
    ters by Charles and Clifford Lanier, as well as tributes by
    Father Tabb, Joel Chandler Harris, Daniel Coit Gilman and
    others.

3   L., C. "Sidney Lanier," in Magazine of Verse. Vol. II.
    Edited by Charles Wells Moulton. Buffalo, New York,
    pp. 253–259.
        Provides a brief biography of Lanier.

4   SLADEN, DOUGLAS. "Some Younger American Poets." Independent,
    XLII (12 June), 806.
        Discovers Lanier had a "pathetic loftiness of purpose,"
    which, blended to the beauty and originality of his poetry
    made him the first Southern poet contributing poetry of
    real value.

1891 A BOOKS - NONE

1891 B SHORTER WRITINGS

1   TURNBULL, FRANCESE L. "Sidney Lanier: A Study," in Younger
    American Poets. Edited by Douglas Sladen. New York:
    Griffith, Farran, Okeden and Welsh, pp. 635–644.
        Finds a "oneness of purpose" in the way ideals shaped his
    work to produce "unfailing loftiness of his aspirations."
    The marsh poems show "evidence of a breadth of scientific
    thought that is cosmic." Suggests the "true keynote and
    master-tone" of his work is "the holiness of beauty." Quali-
    ties of his genius are: "wealth of imagination"; "powers of
    poetic conception"; "art in the coining of happy phrases";
    "deft marshalling of vowels and consonants"; "union of close
    study and broad reading with deep poetic insight"; "the
    finest flushes of poetic feeling, and the most daring

1891

> freedom in the use of passionate, thought-laden outbursts
> of expression"; and quick, full, and unvarying reliance
> upon intuition and the intuitive perception of great truth
> as the poet's supremest gift.

2   WARD, WILLIAM HAYES. "Memorial," in <u>The Poems of Sidney
    Lanier</u>. Edited by Mary Day Lanier. New York: Scribner's,
    pp. xi-xli.
>   Reprint of 1884.B7.

1892 A BOOKS - NONE

1892 B SHORTER WRITINGS

1   BASKERVILL, WILLIAM. "Southern Literature." <u>Publications of
    the Modern Language Association</u>, VII:89-100.
>   Feels that Georgia avoided the South's artificiality.
>   In Lanier the South gained "literary fellowship with the
>   world."

2   KENT, CHARLES. "A Study of Lanier's Poems." <u>Publications of
    the Modern Language Association</u>, VII (April), 33-63.
>   Lanier was a "true poet" for his intensity of love and
>   fullness of artistic aspirations.

3   ROYCE, JOSIAH. <u>Spirit of Modern Philosophy</u>. Boston:
    Houghton Mifflin, pp. 442-445.
>   Uses the example of Lanier's "How Love Looked for Hell"
>   to show that to him evil was illusory. Royce believes this
>   to be "the deepest essence of religion."

4   STEDMAN, EDMUND CLARENCE. "The Nature and Elements of Poetry."
    <u>Century Magazine</u>, XXII (October), 859-869.
>   Since Lanier tried to lead the lives of poet, painter
>   and musician, his work ultimately was "merely tentative
>   from his own point of view."

5   TRENT, WILLIAM P. <u>William Gilmore Simms</u>. Boston: Houghton
    Mifflin, pp. 442-445.
>   Like Lanier, Simms failed to exercise "proper control"
>   on his imagination.

1893 A BOOKS - NONE

1893 B SHORTER WRITINGS

1   ANON. Notice of a Lanier lecture. <u>Critic</u>, XXIII (5 August),
    95.
        Discovered through Lanier that Southern poets were less
    Puritan and more spontaneous and ideal than Northern poets.

2   GOSSE, EDMUND. "Has America Produced a Poet?", in <u>Questions</u>
    <u>at Issue</u>. London: H. Heinemann, pp. 71-90.
        Arguing that no reasonable critic can call him the great
    American poet, finds that Lanier on all occasions "substi-
    tuted vague, cloudy rhetoric for passion; and tortured fancy
    for imagination, always striving, against the grain, to say
    something unparalleled." Reprint of 1888.B6.

3   SLADEN, DOUGLAS. "An American Rossetti." <u>Literary World</u>
    (London), XLVIII (17 November), 378-379.
        Observes distant similarities in the fact that Rossetti
    was a landscape painter and Lanier a nature poet whose
    "Marshes of Glynn" may be the greatest poem by an American.

1894 A BOOKS - NONE

1894 B SHORTER WRITINGS

1   CONWAY, MONCURE D. "Mr. Conway and the Washington-Lanier-Ball
    Tradition." <u>William and Mary College Quarterly Historical</u>
    <u>Magazine</u> (Williamsburg, Virginia), III (October), 137-139.
        Provides a detailed record of Lanier's relations. <u>See</u>
    1894.B2 and 1895.B9.

2   HAYDEN, HORACE E. "Lanier-Washington-Ball." <u>William and Mary</u>
    <u>College Quarterly Historical Magazine</u> (Williamsburg,
    Virginia), III (July), 71-74.
        Similar to 1894.B1. <u>See</u> 1895.B9.

3   LINK, S. A. "Pioneers of Southern Literature." <u>New England</u>
    <u>Magazine</u> (Boston), X (March), 14-19.
        Contends that Lanier needed a longer life to gain rank
    among the great writers.

4   RUTHERFORD, MILDRED. "Sidney Lanier," in <u>American Authors</u>.
    Atlanta, Georgia: Franklin, pp. 368-375.
        Finds that Lanier is admired as the best poet since the
    New England poets, partly because of his integration of

extensive reading, wide interests, and sensitivity to nature. Revised: 1906.B10.

5   SIMONDS, ARTHUR B. <u>American Song</u>. New York: Putnam's, pp. 122–125.
        Notes that Lanier's power of imagination, especially in "The Marshes of Glynn," ranks him with Longfellow.

6   SPANN, MINNIE. "Sidney Lanier's Youth." <u>Independent</u>, XLVI (21 June), 789.
        Finds that as a youth Lanier exhibited dignity, honor and dedication in his college work, as well as devotion to music. He also showed loyalty to the South in war and to his brother and family in peace, while eliciting the affection of Father Tabb.

7   _____. "Sidney Lanier's Manhood." <u>Independent</u>, LXVI (28 June), 821–822.
        Describes the life and work of Lanier's maturity, stressing his spiritual growth.

8   THAYER, WILLIAM R. "Letters of Sidney Lanier." <u>Atlantic</u>, LXXIV (July), 14–28.
        Provides an over-view of the plight of the artist in the modern mercantile world, focusing on how Lanier's suffering in this situation outweighed that of the New England poets or Poe. Supplies a brief description of the support Peacock gave Lanier in publishing "Corn." Revised: 1899.B22. <u>See</u> 1945.B2.

9   _____. "Letters of Sidney Lanier." <u>Atlantic</u>, LXXIV (August), 181–193.
        Provides a brief description of Lanier's reliance upon Peacock in his illness, and of his travel to Florida. Reprinted: 1899.B22. <u>See</u> 1945.B2.

1895 A BOOKS – NONE

1895 B SHORTER WRITINGS

1   ALLEN, ALFRED. "Reminiscences of Sidney Lanier." <u>Mid-Continent Magazine</u> (Louisville, Kentucky), VI (May), 81–86.
        Recalls that once in a Florida hotel he mentioned that he knew Lanier's sons, and a woman there remarked that she knew Lanier and helped liberate him from captivity during the Civil War.

2 BASKERVILL, WILLIAM M. "Some Appreciations of Sidney Lanier."
      <u>Dial</u>, XVIII (16 May), 299-301.
         Review of Callaway, <u>The Select Poems of Sidney Lanier</u>
      1895.B4. Praises Callaway's editorial taste, insight, and
      discrimination. Contends that although Lanier's life was
      a true poem, he lacked simplicity, spontaneity, individual-
      ity, passion and perfection.

3 BEERS, HENRY A. <u>Studies in American Letters</u>. Philadelphia:
      George W. Jacobs, p. 212.
         Finds that Lanier's division of interest between music
      and poetry hampered his originality, though he produced
      some of the most typically Southern poetry.

4 CALLAWAY, MORGAN. "Introduction," in his <u>Select Poems of</u>
      <u>Sidney Lanier</u>. New York: Scribner's, pp. xiii-lv.
         Contends that Lanier offered solutions to the chief
      problems of his Age, through music, nature and, above all,
      love. Credits Lanier with making a synthesis of scientific
      and moral thought.

5 GOODWIN, GRACE DUFFIELD. "Lanier and Keats." <u>Independent</u>,
      XLVII (29 August), 1154.
         Like Keats, Lanier had a light, fine touch and was "over-
      languaged," though unlike Keats, Lanier had a broader sweep
      and unity of soul through his merger of love and knowledge.

6 KING, FRED ALWIN. "Sidney Lanier: Poet, Critic, and
      Musician." <u>Sewanee Review</u>, III (February), 216-30.
         Traces Lanier's tripartite roles of poet, critic and mu-
      sician to his youthful enthusiasms in reading and personal
      experiences.

7 LANIER, CLIFFORD A. "Reminiscences of Sidney Lanier."
      <u>Chautauquan</u>, XXI (July), 403-409.
         Recounts anecdotes from his life with his brother, ex-
      plaining the significance of his reading Scott, German
      writers, and British poets.

8 MANLY, LOUISE. <u>Southern Literature from 1579-1895</u>. Richmond,
      Virginia: B. F. Johnson, pp. 394-398.
         Provides a biographical sketch into which segments of
      later poems are interwoven.

9 TYLER, LYON G. "Lanier-Ball." <u>William and Mary College</u>
      <u>Quarterly Historical Magazine</u>, IV (July), 35-36.
         Examines Lanier's geneology. <u>See</u> 1894.B1, 1894.B2.

1895

10   WARD, WILLIAM HAYES. "Memorial," in The Poems of Sidney
       Lanier. Edited by Mary Day Lanier. New York: Scribner's,
       pp. xi–xli.
            Reprint of 1884.B7.

1896 A BOOKS - NONE

1896 B SHORTER WRITINGS

1   PATTEE, FRED LEWIS. A History of American Literature.
       New York: Silver, Burdett, pp. 389–391.
            Considers music to have been of most importance to
       Lanier, and poetry merely one of its many varieties. Re-
       marks, "he set out in all seriousness to compose symphonies
       in words."

1897 A BOOKS - NONE

1897 B SHORTER WRITINGS

1   ANON. "Sidney Lanier." Critic, XXXI (24 July), 45.
            Reviews Baskervill's Southern Writers 1897.B2. Agrees
       with Baskervill that Lanier "must rank among the intentional,
       the intellectual poets." Reviewer contends Lanier could
       never have written great poetry because of his belief in
       the identity of poetry and music as indicated in his letters.

2   BASKERVILL, WILLIAM M. "Sidney Lanier," in his Southern
       Writers. New York: Gordian Press, pp. 137–298.
            Knits letters, reminiscences, and notes from Lanier's
       friends into a biographical essay which pursues Lanier's
       "philosophic and scientific mind." Traces three stages in
       Lanier's development: a rigid, overwrought apprenticeship;
       a simple, spontaneous phase; and a powerful, musical conclu-
       sion. Toward the end he made "marvelous progress" toward
       giving perfect poetic expression to his scientific theories.

3   BATES, KATHARINE LEE. American Literature. New York:
       Macmillan, pp. 188–190.
            Suggests similarities between Tiger-Lilies and Longfel-
       low's Hyperion, as well as between Poe's view of poetry as
       "rhythmic beauty" and Lanier's practices.

4   GOODWIN, GRACE D. "Two Singers of Sunrise: Lanier, Gilder."
       Poet-Lore, IX (Summer), 407–410.
            Gilder's "New Day" reveals "pure and spontaneous joy in
       beauty," but Lanier's "Sunrise" etherealized nature.

5   LANIER, MARY DAY. "Prefatory Note," in The English Novel.
       New York: Scribner's, pp. v–vii.
          Explains that Lanier's original title for this book,
       "From Aeschylus to George Eliot: The Development of Per-
       sonality," was closer to his intentions, since Lanier meant
       to chart spiritual changes not literary progress.

6   WARD, WILLIAM HAYES. "Four Poems." Independent, XLIX
       (22 July), 933.
          Discusses "Clover," "The Crystal," "A Ballad of Trees
       and the Master," and "Sunrise"--four poems of a dozen sent
       to him for publication when Ward edited the Independent.
       "Clover" evoked "wonder" at its strangeness. "The Crystal"
       sent sudden electric flashes through him. "A Ballad of
       Trees and the Master" sounded tender as the hushed harps
       of angels. "Sunrise" struck him as a poem for poets.

7   WYSHAM, HENRY CLAY. "Sidney Lanier." Independent, LXIX
       (18 November), 1489–1490.
          Collects several strands of interest about Lanier--his
       symmetrical physical traits, his passion for music, the sad
       quality of his humor, and his German connections.

1898 A BOOKS - NONE

1898 B SHORTER WRITINGS

1   BENTZON, THERESE (Mme Blanc). "A Poet-Musician, Sidney
       Lanier." Littell's Living Age (Boston), CCXVII (14 May),
       411–423.
          Biographical notes concerning Lanier's Baltimore experi-
       ences. Translated from the French.

2   _____. "A Poet-Musician, Sidney Lanier." Littell's Living
       Age (Boston), CCXVII (21 May), 517–524.
          Continuation of 1898.B1.

3   LANIER, HENRY W. "Preparatory Note," in Music and Poetry.
       New York: Scribner's, pp. vii–viii.
          Proclaims that his father wrote these essays from a
       "lofty" view of the unity of all the arts.

4   NOBLE, CHARLES. "Sidney Lanier." Studies in American
       Literature. New York: Macmillan, pp. 268–277.
          Avers that poetry to Lanier was a sacred power, used only
       for the highest ends, as in "The Symphony." Considers that
       the nature poems show an ultimate mastery of "the possible
       modulations of sound."

1898

5   PANCOAST, HENRY S. <u>An Introduction to American Literature</u>.
    New York: Henry Holt, pp. 275–283.
        In comparing Lanier to Poe, indicates that Lanier was
    more dedicated to morality and all his experiments were de-
    veloped for this end. He therefore pointed the way to a
    more passionate poetry than that of the New England poets.
    But Lanier's lofty conception of art placed grave demands
    on his strength, exacerbated by circumstances. Hence, his
    experiments are difficult to evaluate, since he needed more
    time to clarify his aims.

6   PERINE, GEORGE C. <u>The Poets and Verse-Writers of Maryland</u>.
    Cincinnati, Ohio: The Editor Publishing Co., pp. 263–267.
        This biographical headnote forms an introduction to "The
    Marshes of Glynn," which Lanier wrote while living in
    Baltimore.

7   SMITH, C. ALPHONSO. "The Possibilities of the South in
    Literature." <u>Sewanee Review</u>, VI (July), 298–305.
        Charts the "New Movement" in Southern literature from
    1875 when Lanier first gained national importance for a
    Southerner with "Corn." Southern writers have since then
    "contributed the most noteworthy portion of American litera-
    ture since 1870."

1899 A BOOKS – NONE

1899 B SHORTER WRITINGS

1   ANON. Review of <u>Music and Poetry</u>. <u>Nation</u>, LXVIII (23 March),
    228.
        Cites suggestive comments on program music, the use of
    the flute and the potential of women as composers.

2   ANON. Review of <u>Music and Poetry</u>. <u>Critic</u>, XXXIV (April),
    365–366.
        Notes that to Lanier music was a refuge from the world
    of facts and science. Differs about the relation of art
    and thought; to Lanier they are complementary; the reviewer
    thinks they are correlative.

3   ANON. Review of <u>Retrospects and Prospects</u>. <u>Independent</u>, LI
    (29 June), 1763.
        Finds that all these essays glow with Lanier's peculiar
    enthusiasm. "The Confederate Memorial Address" is a "prose
    poem of remarkable fervor and dignity."

4   ANON. Review of Retrospects and Prospects. Chautauquan, XXIX
      (August), 512.
           Indicates that Lanier's prose contains "beauties."

5   ANON. Review of Lanier's Letters. Nation, LXIX (30 November),
      416.
           Observes that Lanier was "a sheet of pure flame" in his
      letters to Bayard Taylor, and that we tend to pardon his
      remarks on Mozart when we read how much Beethoven meant to
      him. The apparently chaotic arrangement of the letters is
      ultimately satisfying since it provides emphasis on coherent
      groupings.

6   BURTON, RICHARD E. "Sidney Lanier's Essays." Book Buyer,
      XVIII (March), 144–145.
           Review of Music and Poetry. Attests that although the
      essays are incomplete, they are not shallow. Acknowledges
      Lanier's grasp of fundamental distinctions of criticism and
      his insistence on high principles.

7   FURST, CLYDE. "Concerning Sidney Lanier." Modern Language
      Notes, XVI (November), 197–205.
           Makes connections between Lanier and other poets--Poe,
      Whitman, Longfellow, Keats and Shakespeare among them--in
      order to show his admiration for Lanier's recent work.

8   HAYNE, PAUL HAMILTON. Introduction to "A Poet's Letters to a
      Friend," in The Letters of Sidney Lanier. Edited by Henry
      Wysham Lanier. New York: Scribner's, pp. 219–221, 223–224,
      225, 242.
           Reprint of 1886.B1, B2.

9   HIGGINSON, THOMAS WENTWORTH. "Sidney Lanier," in his
      Contemporaries. Boston: Houghton Mifflin, pp. 85–101.
           Reprint of 1887.B4.

10   LANIER, CHARLES DAY. "Preface," in his Bob: The Story of Our
      Mocking-Bird. New York: Scribner's, pp. vi–viii.
           Describes the experiences which prompted Lanier's poem,
      "The Mocking-Bird."

11   _____. "Prefatory Note," in The Letters of Sidney Lanier.
      Edited by Henry Wysham Lanier. New York: Scribner's,
      pp. vii–ix.
           Aims to provide a "closer glimpse of Lanier the man" and
      reveal the special union of poetry and music in Lanier's
      thought.

12   _____. "Prefatory Note," in his <u>Retrospects and Prospects</u>.
New York: Scribner's, pp. v-vii.
      Justifies this assemblage of Sidney Lanier's essays by
their practical good sense and recurrent hopefulness.

13 LANIER, HENRY WYSHAM. "Letters Between Two Poets." <u>Atlantic</u>,
LXXXIII (June), 791–807.
      Supplies a headnote and remarks between the letters from
Lanier to Bayard Taylor and from Taylor to Lanier, 1875–
1876.
      Henry Wysham Lanier details how Lanier met Taylor through
Gibson Peacock's enthusiasm for "The Symphony." Details how
Lanier met Taylor at a time when Taylor had risen from his
own obscurity with his <u>Faust</u> translation. Taylor's efforts
on behalf of Lanier, culminating in Taylor's successful support for Lanier as writer of the "Centennial Cantata," are
described. Revised: 1899.B14.

14   _____. "Letters Between Two Poets," in his <u>The Letters of
Sidney Lanier</u>. New York: Scribner's, pp. 119–120.
      Revision of 1899.B13. Henry Wysham Lanier deletes all
notes to the letters formerly between various letters, and
he also deletes from the headnote a paragraph describing
Lanier's excitement over the impending initial meeting with
Taylor.

15   _____. "Letters Between Two Poets." <u>Atlantic</u>, LXXXIV (July),
127–141.
      Supplies a brief note to the letters between Lanier and
Taylor 1877–1878, describing the aftermath of the "Centennial Cantata" and the upswing in Lanier's career created by
the publication of <u>Poems</u>. Revised: 1899.B16.

16   _____. "Letters Between Two Poets," in his <u>The Letters of
Sidney Lanier</u>. New York: Scribner's, pp. 169–170.
      In this introductory note, retains the same remarks, but
supplies a date for one letter, while changing the date of
another, thereby shifting it from correct chronological
sequence. Revision of 1899.B15.

17   _____. "A Poet's Musical Impressions." <u>Scribner's</u>, XXV (May),
622–623.
      Supplies a brief note to letters from Lanier mainly to
Mary Day Lanier 1869–1874. Henry Wysham Lanier notes
Lanier's "eager suspense" when he first heard "really great
orchestral music." At this time Lanier began to receive
support for his intuition that his "strongest impulse" was
toward music. Reprinted: 1899.B18.

18 _____. "A Poet's Musical Impressions," in his The Letters of
Sidney Lanier. New York: Scribner's, p. 65.
　　　Rearranges one letter, making it into two letters and
dating the newly created letter. Reprint of 1899.B17.

19 _____. "A Poet's Musical Impressions." Scribner's, XXV
(June), 745–752.
　　　Collects letters to Mary Day Lanier 1874–1876. Re-
printed: 1899.B20.

20 _____. "A Poet's Musical Impressions," in his The Letters of
Sidney Lanier. New York: Scribner's, pp. 97–116.
　　　Alters the dating of one letter.

21 PAYNE, WILLIAM MORTON. Review of Music and Poetry. Dial
(Chicago), XXVI (16 May), 338–339.
　　　Agrees with Lanier that music is not only the measure of
a perfect art, but a moral agent as well.

22 THAYER, WILLIAM R. "Introduction" to "The Letters of Sidney
Lanier to Mr. Gibson Peacock," in The Letters of Sidney
Lanier. Edited by Henry Wysham Lanier. New York:
Scribner's, pp. 3–9.
　　　Revision of 1894.B8. Reprint of 1894.B9. In his re-
vised "Introduction," Thayer deletes his general remarks on
the plight of the nineteenth-century poet.

23 WILLS, GEORGE S. "Sidney Lanier--His Life and Writings."
Publications of the Southern Historical Association, III
(July), 190–211.
　　　Gives a brief biography with a bibliography.

1900 A BOOKS - NONE

1900 B SHORTER WRITINGS

1 ANON. "Intimate Letters of Sidney Lanier." Dial, XXVIII
(16 January), 55.
　　　Concludes that "the man shows larger than the poet," for
Lanier had "delicate sympathy and fine nobility of character."

2 H., M. L. "Sidney Lanier--a Sketch." Modern Culture, XII
(September), 8–9.
　　　A biographical sketch emphasizing inspirational aspects
of Lanier's life.

1900

3   KELL, JOHN M. <u>Recollections of a Naval Life</u>. Washington:
      Neale, pp. 296–297.
         Recounts Lanier's enthusiastic walk through a corn field
      prior to writing "Corn," and said of Lanier's flute-playing,
      "the very soul of the master seemed to breathe out in its
      heavenly cadences."

4   LE GALLIENNE, RICHARD. "Sidney Lanier." <u>Academy</u> (London),
      LVIII (17 February), 147–148.
         Finds that Lanier's flute explains his "History, tempera-
      ment and gift," and that no one has ever equalled Lanier's
      translation into verse of "the ecstasy of modern man as he
      stands and beholds the sunrise." Reprinted in 1900.B5.

5   ____. "Poetry of Lanier." <u>Living Age</u> (Boston), CCXXIV
      (31 March), 840–843.
         Reprint of 1900.B4.

6   McCOWAN, HERVEY SMITH. "Sidney Lanier, The Southern Singer,
      and His Songs." <u>Self Culture</u>, X (January), 398–400.
         Argues that "it is impossible to understand the basic
      principles of Sidney Lanier's poetry without a knowledge of
      his passionate, divine insight into music."

7   SNODDY, JAMES S. "Color and Motion in Lanier." <u>Poet-Lore</u>
      (Philadelphia), XII (Autumn), 558–570.
         Itemizes color, motion, and color-motion imagery, con-
      tending that no poet exceeds Lanier in his use of color.

8   WENDELL, BARRETT. <u>Literary History of America</u>. New York:
      Scribner's, pp. 495–499.
         Suggests that the passion provoked in the South by the
      Civil War created Lanier's unique lyric power.

9   WOOLF, W. P. "Sidney Lanier as Revealed in His Letters."
      <u>Sewanee Review</u>, VIII (July), 346–364.
         Interlaces extracts from Lanier's letters with poems of
      the same period. Notes that Lanier's fame is "upon a cres-
      cendo wave" now that his poems and letters have both been
      published. Finds the letters poetic; groups of them tell
      stories.

<u>1901 A BOOKS - NONE</u>

<u>1901 B SHORTER WRITINGS</u>

1   DABNEY, JULIA P. <u>The Musical Basis of Verse</u>. New York:
      Longman's, Green, passim.

Frequently cites Lanier as an authoritative source for many matters of prosody. Reprinted: 1968.B1.

2 ONDERDONK, JAMES L. History of American Verse: 1610-1897. Chicago: A. C. McClurg, pp. 356-358.
Argues that Lanier was Whitman's antithesis, since he subordinated the physical to the spiritual.

3 SWIGGETT, GLEN LEVIN. "Sidney Lanier." Conservative Review (Washington), V (September), 187-192.
Pleads for a serious estimation of Lanier.

1902 A BOOKS - NONE

1902 B SHORTER WRITINGS

1 GILMAN, DANIEL COIT. "The Launching of a University." Scribner's, XXXI (March), 327-336.
Fits Lanier's tenure at Johns Hopkins into this depiction of the growth of the university.

2 _____. "Pleasant Incidents of an Academic Life." Scribner's, XXXI (May), 614-624.
Recalls the tributes at the celebration of Lanier's forty-sixth birthday, over which Gilman presided. Lanier went through Johns Hopkins like a comet, and he possessed a "poetic fire" that "nothing could quench."

3 LANIER, HENRY W. "Preface," in his edition of Shakspere and His Forerunners. New York: Doubleday, pp. vii-x.
Suggests that Lanier's insight came from "real passion" withheld from scholars. His notes show that this most ambitious prose of his was to lead to his study of George Eliot and the development of modern personality.

4 MABIE, HAMILTON. "The Poetry of the South." International Monthly (Burlington, Vermont), V (February), 201-223.
Argues that Lanier's "lyrical attitude toward nature and life" and his valuation of "feeling rather than intellect" typified Southern poets. But because he sought a relation of poetry to music as well as a "sense of spaciousness" united to "the freedom of great ideas," he developed a quality of imagination surpassing Emerson and linking him to Shakespeare.

5 SHEPHERD, HENRY E. "Sidney Lanier." Current Literature, XXXII (January), 108-111.

1902

        Contends that in different circumstances Lanier would have ranged "among the supreme masters" of "musical interpretation."

6   WOOLF, WINFIELD P. "The Poetry of Sidney Lanier." Sewanee Review, X (July), 325-340.

        Refutes the notion that concern for science and music weakened his work.

1903 A BOOKS - NONE

1903 B SHORTER WRITINGS

1   ANON. Review of Shakspere and His Forerunners. Nation, LXXVI (14 May), 401.

        Finds that although filled with minor errors and containing unproven assumptions, his book shows enthusiasm for the sonneteers and his insight into the metrical order of Shakespeare's plays "quite carries one away."

2   ANON. "Lanier's 'Shakspere and His Forerunners.'" Outlook, LXXIV (20 June), 475-477.

        Discovers "rich nuggets" within a great deal of "low-grade ore." Despite defects in the overall plan, contains acute suggestions—primarily in the analogy between musical harmony and moral wisdom shown in the development of Shakespeare's work.

3   BURTON, RICHARD. Literary Leaders of America. New York: Chautauqua Press, pp. 296-309.

        Insists that although like Tennyson Lanier was a "true song writer," he sacrificed lucidity for spiritual force.

4   FEW, W. P. "Sidney Lanier as Student of English Literature." South Atlantic Quarterly, II (April), 157-168.

        Review of Shakspere and His Forerunners. Though useless to the serious critic and unsafe for the amateur, these essays throw light on Lanier's interest in critical method and the way he turned to the past to understand the present.

5   GREENSLET, FERRIS. "Lanier's Lectures on Shakespeare." Atlantic, XCI (February), 266-267.

        Contends that while Lanier is too often inaccurate and has "no real grasp and coordination of the intellectual forces at play" before Shakespeare's time, yet the volume is justified because it shows "the working of a truly poetic imagination."

6   HEINEMANN, W. Review of Shakspere and His Forerunners.
    Athenaeum (London), no. 3943 (23 May), pp. 649-650.
         Argues that Lanier's work suffers from being unrevised
    and for containing extempore material from lectures. De-
    spite frequent factual and interpretative errors, places
    importance on form and indicates the relation of music to
    verse.

7   HENNEMAN, JOHN BELL. "The National Element in Southern
    Literature." Sewanee Review, XI (July), 345-366.
         Maintains that Lanier's work anticipated modern develop-
    ments--the dialect poems and Tiger Lilies forecasted real-
    ism, if genuinely romantic, while Lanier kept romanticism
    alive in the South at the moment when Southern provincial-
    ism began to die.

8   LANIER, CLIFFORD. "Sidney Lanier." Gulf States Historical
    Magazine (Montgomery, Alabama), II (July), 9-17.
         Recounts the life of his "consecrated" brother Sidney,
    stressing traits inherited from relatives, and retelling
    Lanier's eager response to early influences at school.

9   OMOND, THOMAS S. English Metrists. Cambridge, Massachusetts:
    R. Felton, pp. 108-109.
         Advises careful, cautious study of The Science of English
    Verse. Treated in more detail in revised edition, 1907.B6.

10 PAINTER, F. V. N. Poets of the South. New York: American
    Book, pp. 81-101, 227-234.
         Though Lanier's genius was primarily musical, The Science
    of English Verse was not intended to impose laws on poets.
    Rather, Lanier reached an "unsurpassable poetic and musical
    rapture," which can be detected in several poems.

11 PAYNE, L. W., JR. "Sidney Lanier's Lectures." Sewanee Review,
    XI (October), 452-462.
         Review of Shakspere and His Forerunners. Commends
    Lanier's enthusiasm for scholarship and authoritative re-
    marks on Shakespeare's use of music. Observes that revision
    would have excised Lanier's personality from the lectures.

12 TOLMAN, ALBERT H. "Shakespeare Criticism and Discussion."
    Dial (Chicago), XXXV (16 September), 165-169.
         Although the essays are discursive and redundant, Lanier
    provides a fine analysis of the sonnet and the insight that
    the sonnet should be a small drama. Credits Lanier with a
    fine grasp of Elizabethan music, and a perceptive awareness
    of changes in Shakespeare's versification.

1903

13   WEBB, WILLIAM. "Southern Poetry: 1849–1881." <u>South Atlantic
     Quarterly</u>, II (April), 35–50.
         Fits Lanier's poetry into the context of other poetry
     written in his time in the South.

14   WEBER, WILLIAM L. <u>Southern Poets</u>. New York: Macmillan,
     pp. xxvii–xxxii.
         Gives a general survey of Lanier's work.

<u>1904 A BOOKS – NONE</u>

<u>1904 B SHORTER WRITINGS</u>

1   ABERNETHY, J. W. <u>Southern Poets: Lanier, Timrod, Hayne</u>.
    New York: Maynard, Merrill, pp. 3–34.
        Lanier overly-intensified his verse with music because
    of his reliance on the theories he propounded in <u>The Science
    of English Verse</u>. Gives extensive annotations to selected
    poems.

2   BURT, MARY E. "Preface" and other notes in her <u>The Lanier
    Book</u>. New York: Scribner's, pp. vii–x, 127–143.
        Collects eight poems and various prose pieces, some
    printed for the first time, in this juvenile volume. Con-
    tends in the "Preface" that Lanier was himself in touch with
    children and childhood, "the strenuous and chivalrous heart
    of boys." He himself was a "Heart-Knight."

3   CLAY-CLOPTON, VIRGINIA. <u>A Belle of the Fifties</u>. New York:
    Doubleday, Page, pp. 197–199, 201.
        Reminisces about her relation to Lanier.

4   MORE, PAUL ELMER. <u>Shelburne Essays: First Series</u>. New York:
    Putnam's Sons, pp. 103–121.
        Asserts that <u>The Science of English Verse</u> is "unexcep-
    tional as a study of the <u>ideal</u> or <u>model</u> verse, but fails to
    consider the variance between the <u>ideal</u> and the <u>actual</u>
    rhythm."

5   MOULTON, CHARLES W. "Sidney Lanier." <u>Library of Literary
    Criticism</u>. Vol. VII. New York: Henry Malkan, pp. 325–332.
        Provides extracts from many writers who comment on
    Lanier's life and work, including: Hayne, Baskervill,
    Blanc, Le Gallienne, and Tabb.

6   PAYNE, WILLIAM MORTON. <u>American Literary Criticism</u>.
    New York: Longman's, Green, pp. 29–30.

Suggests that poetic insights compensated for lack of academic training in Lanier's criticism. Yet he forced the relationship between music and poetry in his poetry as well as in The Science of English Verse.

7   SNODDY, JAMES S. "Sidney Lanier: The Poet of Sunrise." Poet-Lore (Philadelphia), XV (Winter), 89–94.
    The usual sense of strain in his poetry departs in his sunrise poems. Lanier leaves interpretation to us.

8   THOMSON, WILLIAM. The Basis of English Rhythm. Glasgow: W. & R. Holmes, pp. 26, 36–38.
    Finds the concept of quantity as the sole basis of rhythm to be untenable, and Lanier's system of notation to be inconsistent because he refuses to admit trochees at the end of pentameter lines.

9   TRENT, WILLIAM P. A Brief History of American Literature. New York: D. Appleton, pp. 223, 229–232.
    Observes that Lanier's life and career reveal a "true scholar and poet...a brave man."

1905 A BOOKS

1   MIMS, EDWIN. Sidney Lanier. Boston: Houghton Mifflin, 375pp.
    Relies heavily on Lanier's letters in stressing his modernity. But the advances made in "The Marshes of Glynn" and The Science of English Verse were stymied by a lack of catholicity directly connected to his weak health and short life. Reprinted in 1968.A1.

1905 B SHORTER WRITINGS

1   ANON. "The Book of a Hero." Outlook, LXXXI (18 November), 650–652.
    Reviews 1905.A1.

2   GILMAN, DANIEL COIT. "Sidney Lanier: Reminiscences and Letters." South Atlantic Quarterly, IV (April), 115–122.
    Recalls the appearance of "The Centennial Cantata," calling it a "noble conception, nobly rendered." Recounts their correspondence about the relations of music and poetry, and reminisces about the memorial observation of Lanier on his forty-sixth birthday.

1905

3   MINOR, BENJAMIN B. The Southern Literary Messenger: 1834-64.
    . New York: Neale, p. 224.
        Surmises that a sonnet of 1862 may be Lanier's, though
    no signed poems of his are listed in the magazine, even
    though he is listed as a contributor.

4   NORTHRUP, MILTON H. "Sidney Lanier: Recollections and
        Letters." Lippincott's Magazine, LXXV (March), 302-315.
        Supplies several anecdotes from his career.

5   PAGE, CURTIS H. Chief American Poets. Cambridge,
        Massachusetts: The Riverside Press, pp. 650-651.
        Offers notes to seventeen poems and a biographical
    sketch with extensive bibliography. While "Corn" contained
    a failed symphonic structure, "The Symphony" succeeded with
    "real harmonic and symphonic structure throughout." The
    Science of English Verse, however, contains mistaken asser-
    tions.

6   SMILEY, JAMES B. A Manual of American Literature. New York:
        American Book, pp. 253-257.
        Emphasizes his break with stereotypical forms.

7   TAYLOR, MARIE HANSEN. On Two Continents. New York:
        Doubleday, Page, pp. 258-259.
        Recounts the instant, mutual responsiveness of Lanier
    and Bayard Taylor to one another.

8   TRENT, WILLIAM P. Southern Writers. New York: Macmillan,
        pp. 404-407.
        Stresses Lanier's nobility.

1906 A BOOKS

1   SNYDER, HENRY N. Modern Poets and Christian Teaching,
        Sidney Lanier. New York: Eaton and Mains, 132pp.
        Explains that this is not a biography but an attempt to
    read Lanier's spiritual message. This "knight-errant in
    the cause of beauty and truth and holiness" offers a
    "strengthening spiritual tonic" brewed in storm and stress.
    No mystic or dreamer, Lanier believed a noble life produced
    noble art, and he achieved this by keeping the Grail of
    Christ in mind. Thus, "Father, Self, and Love" become his
    creed, and it infuses all his poetry, making it religious.
    He was an apostle of optimism with a gospel of love.

1906 B SHORTER WRITINGS

1   ANON. "Sidney Lanier's Place in American Poetry." Current
     Literature, XL (January), 36–38.
          Reviews 1905.A1.

2   ANON. "Sidney Lanier." Independent, LX (11 January), 109–110.
          Review of Sidney Lanier 1905.A1. Notes that the early
     life shows Lanier was not a "detached" figure, and pleased
     to see that Mims has accurately recorded the importance of
     the Independent in Lanier's career. Observes that although
     Lanier needed more time to revise his work, his imperfection
     pleases more than Poe's perfection.

3   ANON. Review of Mims's Sidney Lanier. Christian Register,
     LXXXV (1 February), 130.
          Contends that Mims proves that Lanier ought to be known
     as a man, not merely through "The Marshes of Glynn," which
     made him immortal. See 1905.A1.

4   CALLAWAY, MORGAN, JR. "Introduction," in Select Poems of
     Sidney Lanier. Edited by the author. New York:
     Scribner's, pp. vii–viii.
          Reprint of 1895.B4.

5   CLARKE, GEORGE H. "Some Early Letters and Reminiscences of
     Sidney Lanier." Independent, LXI (8 November), 1092–1098.
          Describes Lanier's early reading, his relation to his
     brother Clifford, and his war experiences, particularly
     chivalric ones. Reprinted: 1907.A1.

6   GILDER, JEANETTE L. "A Grand Old Man of Science, a Grand Old
     Man of Politics, and a Poet." Critic, XLVIII (April), 355.
          Commends Mims's honesty in stressing that Lanier's worth
     cannot be fixed yet.

7   HENNEMAN, JOHN BELL. "The Biography of Sidney Lanier."
     Sewanee Review, XIV (July), 352–357.
          Review of Mims's Sidney Lanier 1905.A1. Finds too many
     extensive quotes from Lanier's letters and too many sugges-
     tions that Lanier is "an uneven writer whose defects are
     glaring." Notes that Mims is humorless and unimaginative,
     leaving the reader confused about Lanier's importance.

8   HOLLIDAY, CARL. A History of Southern Literature. New York:
     Neale, pp. 343–355.
          Finds Lanier's musical effects "not often equalled," but
     he is unsure if this derives from his Science of English
     Verse theories or not.

1906

9   HUBNER, CHARLES W. <u>Representative Southern Poets</u>. New York:
    Neale, pp. 15-54.
        Cites Lanier's "luminousness of inspiration," and finds
    him "the best celebrant of the ecstasy of modern man before
    the elemental glories of nature." Recounts hearing Lanier
    play his flute.

10 RUTHERFORD, MILDRED L. <u>The South in History and Literature</u>.
    Athens, Georgia: Franklin-Turner, pp. 485-495.
        Cites Lanier's extensive reading, wide scope of inter-
    ests, and religious attitude toward nature in asserting that
    Lanier is considered the best poet since the New England
    writers. A revision of 1894.B4.

11 _____. <u>The South in History and Literature</u>. Athens, Georgia:
    Franklin-Turner, pp. 495-498.
        Notes the collaboration between Clifford Lanier and his
    brother.

12 SCHERER, JAMES A. <u>The Holy Grail</u>. Philadelphia: J. B.
    Lippincott, pp. 73-112.
        Discovers that Lanier's art is superior to Poe's because
    he combines beauty, wisdom, and passion. As a "poet-
    prophet" Lanier was a "clear-eyed seer of the truth." But
    his "throbbing vitality" transforms his poetry. He became
    a "true knight of the Grail" because his basic passion was
    a passion for holiness.

13 SIMONDS, W. E. "Two American Men of Letters." <u>Dial</u>, XL
    (16 February), 119-122.
        Reviews Edwin Mims' <u>Sidney Lanier</u> 1905.A1. Suggests that
    Lanier and James Russell Lowell were akin in "their ideal-
    ity, their sincerity, their intellectuality, and in their
    deep spiritual vision." Credits Mims with picturesqueness,
    naturalness, simplicity, fullness of detail, and dispas-
    sionate discussion of Lanier's rank as a poet.

14 TRAUBEL, HORACE. <u>With Walt Whitman in Camden</u>. Boston:
    Small, Maynard, Vol. I, pp. 170-171, 207, 208, 209; Vol. II,
    pp. 417, 422.
        Records that Whitman felt Lanier used his genius for
    musicality far too much, and that Lanier "made more sound
    than sense." Reproduces Lanier's letter to Whitman.

15 [WHITE, E. L.]. Review of Edwin Mims' <u>Sidney Lanier</u>. <u>Nation</u>,
    LXXXII (18 January), 60.
        Notes that Mims writes with accuracy but without charm,
    but his chief fault is that he does not lure the reader

deeply into an interest in Lanier. Questions his tact,
suggesting that some facts revealed in the letters quoted
from will pain those admiring Lanier and repel those they
should allure. Contends that the gravest problem with the
biography is that the quoted poetry does not support the
generally-held view that Lanier was a great poet, and the
biographer's task was to prove that he was or show why he
was over-valued. See 1905.A1.

1907 A BOOKS

1   CLARKE, GEORGE HERBERT. Some Reminiscences and Early Letters
      of Sidney Lanier. Macon, Georgia: J. W. Burke, 27pp.
        Reprint of 1906.B5.

1907 B SHORTER WRITINGS

1   ATKINSON, C. PRESCOTT. "Clifford Lanier," in Library of
      Southern Literature. Vol. VII. Atlanta, Georgia: Martin
      and Hoyt, pp. 3021–3039.
        Provides a detailed biography of Lanier's brother.

2   DEWEY, THOMAS E. Poetry in Song. Kansas City, Missouri:
      Franklin Hudson, pp. 46–73.
        Examines the prosody of several of Lanier's poems and
      concludes that "his art was unconscious in great degree."

3   FRASER, A. M. "James Woodrow: 1828–1907," in Library of
      Southern Literature. Vol. XIII. Atlanta, Georgia: Martin
      and Hoyt, pp. 5957–5963.
        Offers a sketch of Lanier's most formative teacher.

4   HILL, WALTER B. "Sidney Lanier," in Reminiscences of Famous
      Georgians. Edited by Lucian Knight. Atlanta, Georgia:
      Franklin-Turner, pp. 712–716.
        Sees "Life and Song" as Lanier's self-allegory, and
      praises Lanier as "the old-time bard" and a poet of "pas-
      sionate purity" whose life is a lesson.

5   KNIGHT, LUCIAN. Reminiscences of Famous Georgians. Atlanta,
      Georgia: Franklin-Turner, pp. 533–537.
        Contends that Lanier is "the poet's poet" but not the
      people's poet; hence he resembles Lowell not Longfellow.

6   OMOND, THOMAS S. English Metrists. Oxford: Henry Frowde,
      pp. 177–186.

1907

Examines <u>The Science of English Verse</u> and discovers that Lanier's distinctive note was his discovery that rhythm was the basis of verse. Asserts that the book is mainly valuable for its principles, not its conclusions. Cites Lanier's "erroneous scansions." Reprinted: 1921.B3; 1968.B6. Revision of 1903.B9.

7   SNYDER, HENRY NELSON. "Sidney Lanier," in <u>Library of Southern Literature</u>. Vol. VII. Atlanta, Georgia: Martin and Hoyt, pp. 3041-3045.
     Offers a biography which stresses Lanier's religious heritage. Considers him a poet of enduring rank for the personality and ideals displayed in his work.

8   _____. "The Matter of 'Southern Literature.'" <u>Sewanee Review</u>, XV (April), 218-226.
     Attempts to discern the "Southern mind" through its literature, keeping Lanier implicitly in mind.

9   WAUCHOPE, GEORGE ARMSTRONG. "Dr. Woodrow and Sidney Lanier," in <u>Dr. James Woodrow</u>. Edited by Marion Woodrow. Columbus, South Carolina: R. L. Bryan, pp. 156-165.
     Evaluates the impact of Lanier's most important Oglethorpe teacher upon his poetry.

1908 A BOOKS - NONE

1908 B SHORTER WRITINGS

1   ANON. Review of <u>Poem Outlines</u>. <u>Current Literature</u>, XLV (November), 572.
     These poem outlines reveal that the essence of poetry can be had without melody or rhyme.

2   ANON. Review of <u>Poem Outlines</u>. <u>Independent</u> (New York), LXV (26 November), 1249.
     The poem outlines provide a "peep" at Lanier's "vagrant moods."

3   ANON. "Last Words from Sidney Lanier." <u>Poet-Lore</u> (Philadelphia), XIX (Winter), 482-487.
     Lanier's <u>Poem Outlines</u> "offer us intimacy with a sensitive poetic soul at moments of imaginative seedtime seldom open to any eye."

4   BOWEN, EDWIN WINFIELD. <u>Makers of American Literature</u>. New York: Neale, pp. 348-370.

Provides a biographical sketch and survey of Lanier's major poems, concluding that Lanier is the best Southern post-bellum poet.

5   BREVARD, CAROLINE M. "Sidney Lanier," in Literature of the South. New York: Broadway, pp. 168–88.
       Focuses on Lanier's dedication to scientific accuracy in his poetry and The Science of English Verse. Finds his reputation improving.

6   GREENSLET, FERRIS. Life of T. B. Aldrich. Boston: Houghton Mifflin, pp. 214–215.
       This 1900 letter from Aldrich to E. C. Stedman criticizes Stedman for including Lanier in an anthology of important American poets, since "in point of poetic accomplishment" he was a musician, not a poet, and in the rear rank of poets.

7   HOLLIDAY, CARL. Three Centuries of Southern Poetry. Nashville, Tennessee: M. E. Church, pp. 173–175.
       Provides a biographical sketch.

8   LANIER, HENRY W. "In a Poet's Workshop: Poem Outlines by Sidney Lanier." Century Magazine, LXXVI (October), 847–850.
       Gives some background to Lanier's poem outlines.

9   MACY, JOHN. The Spirit of American Literature. New York: Boni and Liveright, pp. 309–323.
       Ranks Lanier with Whitman and Poe, but feels he never would have written The Science of English Verse had he been free to pursue poetry exclusively. Reprinted in 1913.B2.

10   NEWCOMER, ALPHONSO G. American Literature. Chicago: Scott, Foresman, pp. 272–275.
       While identifying Lanier as a great poet, suggests Lanier lost sight of the boundaries of music and poetry.

11   ORGAIN, KATE ALMA. Southern Authors in Poetry and Prose. New York: Neale, pp. 9–18.
       Offers a brief biographical sketch.

12   SMITH, CHARLES FORSTER. Reminiscences and Sketches. Nashville, Tennessee: M. E. Church, pp. 136–163.
       Recalls Lanier's dedication to music and poetry, lamenting the brevity of his life.

1909

1909 A BOOKS - NONE

1909 B SHORTER WRITINGS

    1   MIMS, EDWIN. Review of <u>Poem Outlines</u>. <u>South Atlantic</u>
        <u>Quarterly</u>, VIII (January), 97-98.
           Asserts that some of these poem outlines ought not to
        have been published, though some of them show Lanier's use
        of epigram and imaginative figures.

1910 A BOOKS

    1   CARROLL, CHARLES C. <u>The Synthesis and Analysis of the Poetry</u>
        <u>of Sidney Lanier</u>. Owensboro, Kentucky: Messenger Job
        Printing, 77pp.
           Blending Biblical quotation with Lanier's main poems,
        Carroll establishes "the preacher's poet" as a superior
        "Light-giver" to his fellow poets. Examines in the first
        six chapters nature, rhythm, wife-love, social conscious-
        ness, "Ego-altruism," and the advocacy of freedom. The
        last seven chapters chart Lanier's growth from his baptism
        in "The Marshes of Glynn" to his "resurrection" as a prophet
        in "Sunrise." At the end, Lanier witnessed "The Light of
        the World" claiming His Kingdom.

1910 B SHORTER WRITINGS

    1   MOSES, MONTROSE J. <u>Literature of the South</u>. New York:
        Thomas Crowell, pp. 268-269, 358-383.
           Finds that "Lanier's sweetest sense of mission" made him
        very conscious of his craft. He became the only "aggressive
        thinker" in the South, reaching through science beyond sec-
        tionalism. He represents the fertility of the New South,
        and thus his consequence to American literature.

    2   ROUTH, JAMES E., JR. "The Poetry of Henry Timrod." <u>South</u>
        <u>Atlantic Quarterly</u>, IX (July), 267-274.
           By comparison to Timrod, Lanier's landscape poetry had
        more scope and deeper passion.

    3   SAINTSBURY, G. E. B. <u>History of English Prosody</u>. Vol. III.
        London: Macmillan, pp. 493-497.
           Disagrees with Omond (1907.B6) that Lanier "firmly es-
        tablished temporal relations as essential to verse," though
        he concurs with Omond that Lanier's scansions are "atro-
        cious." Cites Lanier for his "impertinence" in using only
        musical notations to chart poetic rhythm.

4   STEDMAN, LAURA and GEORGE M. GOULD. <u>Life and Letters of</u>
      <u>Edmund Clarence Stedman</u>. Vol. II. New York: Moffat, Yard,
      pp. 115, 154, and 279.
         Quoting Stedman's 1880 and 1886 letters reveals agree-
      ment with Lanier that poetry is not a science "but there <u>is</u>
      a science of poetry," although Lanier was misled by trying
      to do in poetry what is fit only for music.

5   TRENT, WILLIAM P. "Sidney Lanier," in <u>The Encyclopedia</u>
      <u>Britannica</u>. Eleventh Edition. Cambridge, England:
      Cambridge University Press, pp. 181–182.
         Observes that by some Lanier is considered "hectic," but
      by others he is defended as "the most original and talented
      of modern American poets."

<u>1911 A BOOKS - NONE</u>

<u>1911 B SHORTER WRITINGS</u>

1   BROOKE, C. F. TUCKER. "Deceptive Illustrations." <u>Dial</u>, LI
      (1 October), 245–246.

2   MATTHEWS, BRANDER. <u>A Study of Versification</u>. Boston:
      Houghton Mifflin, pp. 74, 87, and 267.
         Finds that the influence of Poe's theories of verse on
      Lanier are obvious. Uses two items from <u>The Science of</u>
      <u>English Verse</u> favorably.

3   PICKETT, LA SALLE CORBELL. "The Sunrise Poet." <u>Lippincott's</u>
      <u>Magazine</u> (Philadelphia), LXXXVIII (December), 851–858.
         Details aspects of Lanier's private life in Macon and
      Baltimore, as well as his war service.

4   SHEPHERD, HENRY E. <u>The Representative Authors of Maryland</u>.
      New York: Whitehall, pp. 75–87
         Examines Lanier's Maryland connections, concluding that
      his rarest "grace of utterance" is best seen in his "Ode to
      Johns Hopkins University." Feels Lanier's fame will reside
      in his criticism.

5   STEDMAN, EDMUND C. "The Late Sidney Lanier," in his <u>Genius</u>
      <u>and Other Essays</u>. New York: J. R. Osgood, pp. 250–253.
         Reprint of 1881.B10.

1912

1912 A BOOKS - NONE

1912 B SHORTER WRITINGS

1   PICKETT, LA SALLE CORBELL. Literary Hearthstones of Dixie.
     Philadelphia: J. B. Lippincott, pp. 41–65.
        Describes places where Lanier lived, evaluating their
     congeniality to his artistic interests.

2   WARD, WILLIAM HAYES. "Memorial," in The Poems of Sidney
     Lanier. Edited by Mary Day Lanier. New York: Scribner's,
     pp. xi–xli.
        Reprint of 1884.B7.

3   WAYLAND, JOHN W. "Sidney Lanier at Rockingham Springs," in
     his A History of Rockingham County, Virginia. Dayton,
     Virginia: Ruebush–Elkins, pp. 435–436.
        Describes the six weeks in 1879 in which Lanier wrote
     The Science of English Verse at Rockingham Springs. Depicts
     the house Lanier occupied, his furniture, his horseback
     rides, and his friends. Relates a story of a tournament in
     which Lanier addressed the "knights."

1913 A BOOKS - NONE

1913 B SHORTER WRITINGS

1   ANON. "Slighting Southern Literature." Literary Digest, XLVI
     (31 May), 1224–1236.
        Challenges the view that Southern literature is inferior
     to Northern writing, a view presented by a reviewer of
     Brander Matthews's Introduction to the Study of American
     Literature.

2   MACY, JOHN. The Spirit of American Literature. New York:
     Boni and Liveright, pp. 309–323.
        Reprint of 1908.B9.

3   PAYNE, LEONIDAS WARREN, JR. Southern Literary Readings.
     New York: Rand–McNally, pp. 209–213.
        Focuses on Lanier's various non–literary employments
     which provide a context for his poetic creativity.

4   WARD, WILLIAM HAYES. "Memorial," in The Poems of Sidney
     Lanier. Edited by Mary Day Lanier. New York: Scribner's,
     pp. xi–xli.
        Reprint of 1884.B7.

1914 A BOOKS - NONE

1914 B SHORTER WRITINGS

1   BURT, MARY E. "Preface," and other notes in her <u>The Lanier</u>
     <u>Book</u>. New York: Scribner's, pp. vii-x, 127-143.
          Reprint of 1904.B2.

2   CADY, FRANK W. "Writings of Sidney Lanier." <u>South Atlantic</u>
     <u>Quarterly</u>, XIII (April), 156-173.
          Believes the label "immaturity" summarizes Lanier's poet-
     ry, for <u>The Science of English Verse</u> was the start, not the
     end, of his career and "Sunrise" showed promise.

1915 A BOOKS

1   WESTFELDT, GUSTAF R. <u>Fifteen Minutes with Sidney Lanier</u>.
     New Orleans: Meade and Sampsell, 9pp.
          Describes Lanier's penultimate day and praises his op-
     timism, a blend of heart, mind, and hand.

1915 B SHORTER WRITINGS

1   HARMAN, HENRY E. "Sidney Lanier--a Study." <u>South Atlantic</u>
     <u>Quarterly</u>, XIV (October), 301-306.
          Feels that Lanier was distinctly Southern and neglected
     in his own time.

2   WARD, WILLIAM HAYES. "Memorial," in <u>The Poems of Sidney</u>
     <u>Lanier</u>. Edited by Mary Day Lanier. New York: Scribner's,
     pp. xi-xli.
          Reprint of 1884.B6.

1916 A BOOKS - NONE

1916 B SHORTER WRITINGS

1   STRONG, AUGUSTUS HOPKINS. <u>American Poets and Their Theology</u>.
     Philadelphia: Griffith and Rowland, pp. 371-418.
          Comparison of Poe and Lanier reveals that Lanier applied
     his scientific method to poetry to improve its moral con-
     tent. Nevertheless, he failed to link God's holiness and
     love to Christ's cross.

1917

1917 A BOOKS - NONE

1917 B SHORTER WRITINGS

   1   POLLARD, EDWARD B. "The Spiritual Message of Sidney Lanier."
       Homiletic Review, LXXIV (August), 91–95.
          Emphasizes music in Lanier's life in this biographical
       sketch. Finds that Lanier's work proved his contention
       that the poet is "the mocking-bird of the spiritual uni-
       verse."

1918 A BOOKS - NONE

1918 B SHORTER WRITINGS

   1   HARMAN, HENRY E. "A Study of Sidney Lanier's 'The Symphony.'"
       South Atlantic Quarterly, XVII (January), 32–39.
          In treating the poor Lanier reached sublimity.

   2   JONES, HOWARD MUMFORD. "Sidney Lanier," in American Poetry.
       Edited by Percy Boynton. New York: Scribner's,
       pp. 670–675.
          Though monotonous in theme, Lanier's music made him
       interesting.

   3   MILES, DUDLEY. "The New South: Lanier," in The Cambridge
       History of American Literature. Vol. II. Edited by
       William P. Trent, et al. New York: Macmillan, 313–346.
          Though an insightful critic, Lanier relies too much on
       personal responses. However, his moral earnestness led to
       a rapprochement with the North.

   4   VARNEDOE, J. O. "Sidney Lanier: An Appreciation." Georgia
       Historical Quarterly, II (September), 139–144.
          Recalls meeting Lanier at Oglethorpe and describes him
       in detail, identifying him as "a great original," and a
       "poet of poets."

1919 A BOOKS

   1   BROCKMAN, CHARLES JOSEPH. "A Monograph on Sidney Lanier."
       Master's Thesis, Lehigh University.
          Examines the personal and circumstantial restrictions
       which kept Lanier from becoming a great writer. Almost en-
       tirely concerned with the prose, particularly The English
       Novel, concludes that his "moral deductions were always

peculiar, probably due to the biased religious training of
his youth."

1919 B SHORTER WRITINGS

1   BOYNTON, PERCY. History of American Literature. Boston:
    Ginn and Company, pp. 349–358.

2   ELLSWORTH, WILLIAM W. A Golden Age of Authors. New York:
    Houghton Mifflin, pp. 111–112.

3   FOERSTER, NORMAN. "Lanier as a Poet of Nature." Nation,
    CVIII (21 June), 981–983.
        Asserts that he contributed a "musician's feeling for
    nature," using nature images to imply musical effects.

1920 A BOOKS - NONE

1920 B SHORTER WRITINGS

1   BRADFORD, GAMALIEL. "Portrait of Sidney Lanier." North
    American Review, CCXI (June), 805–817.
        Examines Lanier's work in terms of his "struggles."
    Therefore, Bradford prefers "June Dreams in January" to the
    marsh poems. Reprinted in 1922.B1.

2   PERRY, BLISS. A Study of Poetry. Boston: Houghton Mifflin,
    pp. 171–172, 210–211.
        The Science of English Verse is very suggestive.

1921 A BOOKS - NONE

1921 B SHORTER WRITINGS

1   ANON. "Sidney Lanier." The National Cyclopedia of American
    Biography. Vol. II. New York: James White, pp. 438–439.
        Illustrated biographical sketch.

2   LANE, MARY. "Macon: An Historical Retrospect." Georgia
    Historical Quarterly, V (September), 20–34.
        Views the city as formative to Lanier's development.

3   OMOND, THOMAS S. English Metrists. Oxford, England:
    Clarendon Press, pp. 195–202. Reprint of 1907.B6.
        Reprinted in 1968.B6.

1921

4   SAPIR, EDWARD. "The Musical Foundations of Verse." Journal
     of English and Germanic Philology, XX:213–228.
         Though many of the ideas here are related to those of
     Lanier's Science of English Verse, he is not treated speci-
     fically by Sapir.

5   TAPPAN, EVA MARCH. A Short History of England's and America's
     Literature. Boston: Houghton Mifflin, pp. 371–374.
         Lanier's poetry is "never without an underlying truth."

1922 A BOOKS

1   LAMAR, E. DOROTHY BLOUNT. Sidney Lanier: Musician, Poet,
     Soldier. Macon, Georgia: J. W. Burke, 46pp.
         Intends that this "collection of data" and its illustra-
     tions be used to spread knowledge of the Christianity typi-
     fied by this "Catholic spirit."

1922 B SHORTER WRITINGS

1   BRADFORD, GAMALIEL. American Portraits, 1875–1900. Boston:
     Houghton Mifflin, pp. 59–83.
         Reprint of 1920.B1.

2   BROOKS, VAN WYCK. "The Literary Life in America," in
     Civilization in America. Edited by Harold E. Stearns.
     New York: Harcourt, Brace, pp. 179–197.
         Asserts that Lanier's talent was "hopelessly crippled by
     poverty."

3   MENCKEN, H. L. Prejudices: Third Series. New York: Alfred
     Knopf, pp. 152–153.
         The Science of English Verse was "the first intelligent
     book ever published upon the nature and structure of the
     sensuous content of English poetry."

1923 A BOOKS - NONE

1923 B SHORTER WRITINGS

1   ELLERBE, J. E. "Sidney Lanier." Confederate Veteran.
     (Nashville, Tennessee), XXXI (June), 210–211.
         Biographical sketch stressing the inspirational quality
     of Lanier's life and his "holy obligation" to poetry.

2   FOERSTER, NORMAN. <u>Nature in American Literature</u>. New York:
     Macmillan, pp. 221–237.
        Asserts that Lanier's best poems are those treating na-
     ture; he alone among poets treats nature with "a musician's
     feeling." To explain why only Lanier "gives Southern land-
     scape," Foerster reviews Lanier's birds and flowers.

3   WEBER, WILLIAM LANDER. <u>Selections from the Southern Poets</u>.
     New York: Macmillan, pp. xxvii–xxxii.
        Provides a biographical sketch, extracting comments from
     other writers.

<u>1924 A BOOKS – NONE</u>

<u>1924 B SHORTER WRITINGS</u>

1   LOVETT, HOWARD MERIWETHER. "Macon in the War Between the
     States." <u>Confederate Veteran</u>. (Nashville, Tennessee),
     XXXII (January), 20–22.
        Provides background on the "Rifles and Volunteers of
     Macon." Lovett was a war companion of Lanier.

2   _____. "Georgia's Intellectual Center in the Sixties."
     <u>Confederate Veteran</u>. (Nashville, Tennessee), XXXII (March),
     97–98.
        Indicates that Macon was the center of Georgia's "intel-
     lectual nobility" after the Civil War. Lanier's novel
     <u>Tiger-Lilies</u> tells better than any other book the tragic
     story of Southerners during the war.

3   M'MAHON, G. W. "Samuel Knox––A Patriot." <u>Confederate Veteran</u>.
     (Nashville, Tennessee), XXXII (March), 89.
        Knox, a flutist, was a roommate of Lanier's at Ogle-
     thorpe.

4   WEIRICK, BRUCE. <u>From Whitman to Sandburg in American Poetry</u>.
     New York: Macmillan, pp. 73–84.
        Finds Lanier under-rated, since his poetry was optimistic
     despite his tragedies, his attitude was nationalistic de-
     spite the Civil War, and his voice individualized in a
     conformist age.

<u>1925 A BOOKS</u>

1   DIXON, A. CLARENCE. <u>Sidney Lanier, the Johns Hopkins Poet:
     An Appreciation</u>. Baltimore, Maryland: privately published,
     10pp.

1925

Finds that faith in God was the basis of his work. Thus "The Crystal" is the fullest expression of this "old time Southern Christian gentleman."

1925 B SHORTER WRITINGS

1 PHILLIPS, W. B. "Barrett Wendell as Seen by a Southerner." Harvard Alumni Bulletin, XXVII (28 May), 986–989.
   Recalls how he chatted with Dr. Wendell when at Harvard in 1913 about Lanier. Wendell found Lanier "the most genuine lyric power yet produced by an American." Wendell warmly praised the delicate pictures and musical effects of "The Marshes of Glynn," though he found the long sentence which opens the poem a distinct flaw. His other faults were his chivalry which created a reluctance in Lanier to face reality and his musical interests which fostered inarticulateness.

2 THORPE, HARRY COLIN. "Sidney Lanier: A Poet for Musicians." Musical Quarterly (New York), XI (July), 373–82.
   Examines many aspects of Lanier's interest in music: his musicality of verse in "Sunrise"; his poems that were set to music; his own poem "Centennial Cantata" which was fitted "inevitably" to the appropriate musical setting; his musical imagery; and his poems treating Beethoven.

3 WOOD, CLEMENT. "Sidney Lanier: Music Weds Poetry," in Poets of America. New York: E. P. Dutton, pp. 68–81.
   Extensively analyzes the relation between The Science of English Verse and twelve poems. Since society was indifferent to its poets, Lanier paid a high price for being "at heart an essential anarchist."

1926 A BOOKS – NONE

1926 B SHORTER WRITINGS

1 ANON. "Sidney Lanier Commemoration." Johns Hopkins Alumni Magazine (Baltimore, Maryland), XIV (June), 482–505.
   Includes three addresses: "The Spirituality of Lanier" by Lizette W. Reese; "Lanier and the University" by President F. J. Goodnow; and "The Genius of the Modern in Lanier" by Reverend Oliver Huckel, the major address. Reese indicates that Lanier's poetry and his life formed a seamless whole. Goodnow reviews Lanier's "remarkable accomplishments" as a scholar. Huckel traces Lanier's "throbbing, exultant...

life and power" in aspects of his modernism, especially
science. Yet to Lanier the age of science meant the re-
juvenation of art and religion. Involved in modern social
issues, he was a "passionate believer in America" who came
to recognize Whitman as a poetic cousin. In his responses
to music and literature he was part of "the new intellectual
life of the South after the war."

2   COTTMAN, GEORGE S. "James F. D. Lanier." Indiana Magazine of
      History (Indianapolis, Indiana), XXII (June), 194–200.
        Contains information on a distant kin of Lanier.

3   GARBER, BLANCHE G. "The Lanier Family and the Lanier Home."
      Indiana Magazine of History (Indianapolis, Indiana), XXII
      (September), 277–284.
        Concerns the Laniers of Madison, Wisconsin, distant rela-
      tives of Lanier.

4   MIMS, EDWIN. The Advancing South. New York: Doubleday,
      Page, pp. 51–53.
        Recounts Lanier's vision of the New South as a prosperous
      agricultural community with an intimate relation between
      politics, social life, morality and art.

5   MONROE, HARRIET. Poets and Their Art. New York: Macmillan,
      pp. 268–284.
        Acknowledges Lanier's attention to the universality of
      rhythm.

6   REDE, KENNETH. "Lanier's 'Owl Against Robin.'" American
      Collector (Metuchen, New Jersey), III (October), 27–30.
        Reveals that the MS poem shows variations from two other
      published texts, and it raises questions about where the
      variants originated, while comparing the texts.

7   WILLIAMS, STANLEY T. The American Spirit in Letters. Pageant
      of America, no. 11. Edited by Ralph H. Gabriel. New
      Haven, Connecticut: Yale University Press, pp. 255–257.
        Contends that although Lanier was a "true poet," he
      never came to "full maturity."

1927 A BOOKS

1   GRAHAM, PHILIP. "Sidney Lanier's Thought in Relation to that
      of his Age." Ph.D. Dissertation, University of Chicago.
        Examines in detail the intellectual milieu of Lanier's
      work, recording his response to the English poets,

1927

Victorian writers, German Romantics, modern scientists, and
local influences. Concludes that Lanier was in the mainstream of the cultural waters of his time.

1927 B SHORTER WRITINGS

1   MYERS, JAY ARTHUR. Fighters of Fate. Baltimore, Maryland:
The Williams and Wilkins Company, pp. 174-181.
Provides a brief sketch.

1928 A BOOKS - NONE

1928 B SHORTER WRITINGS

1   ANDERSEN, JOHANNES C. The Laws of Verse. London:
Cambridge University Press, pp. 179-180.

2   FLOURNOY, M. H. Essays: Historical and Critical. Baltimore,
Maryland: The Norman Remington Company, pp. 89-96.
Asserts that Lanier had a "stronger hand" than Timrod or
Hayne and "none of Poe's bitterness."

3   HENDRICK, BURTON JESSE. The Training of an American: The
Earlier Life and Letters of Walter H. Page, 1855-1913.
Boston: Houghton Mifflin, p. 325.
While studying at Johns Hopkins he came to know Lanier
as a great poet and fine flutist.

1929 A BOOKS - NONE

1929 B SHORTER WRITINGS

1   ANON. "A Poet-Musician." New York Times (20 September),
Section 3, p. 1.
The cult of Lanier grows in the South, but the nation
should realize he was the first Southern voice "to attract
the ear of the outside world" after the Civil War.

2   GARLAND, HAMLIN. "Roadside Meetings of a Literary Nomad."
Bookman (New York), LXX (December), 403-406.
His enthusiasm for Lanier began with The Science of English Verse. Lanier's lyricism, social sensitivity, and
"cosmic landscapes" were strong early influences. Revised
in 1930.B1.

3   GREENLAW, EDWIN. "A Sidney Lanier Professorship at Johns
       Hopkins." Johns Hopkins Alumni Magazine (Baltimore),
       XVIII (January), 136–141.
          Lanier's interest in pure research and his unpartisan
       criticism of American materialism were fruitful in a uni-
       versity. The new professorship would have great importance
       in the study of the roots of American culture and the de-
       velopment of a creative criticism of the nation, for the
       poet's life inspired these goals.

4   KEYSERLING, HERMANN. "The South—America's Hope." Atlantic,
       CXLIV (November), 605–608.
          Implies that the life and work of Lanier helped to create
       a "superior human type" in the South, giving it a "general
       cultural atmosphere."

5   KREYMBORG, ALFRED. Our Singing Strength. New York: Coward,
       McCann, pp. 160–171.
          Labels Lanier a "didactic regionalist." However, the
       imagery of "The Marshes of Glynn" made Lanier a poet of
       "tragic mystery."

6   PRATT, WALDO S. The New Encyclopedia of Men and Musicians.
       New York: Macmillan, p. 515.
          Outlines his musical career and musical verse.

7   RUSSELL, CHARLES EDWARD. An Hour of American Poetry.
       Philadelphia: J. B. Lippincott, pp. 112–116.
          Points out a "strange analogy" between "The Marshes of
       Glynn" and Swinburne's "Evensong on the Broads."

8   STARKE, AUBREY H. "Sidney Lanier and Paul Hamilton Hayne:
       Three Unpublished Letters." American Literature, I
       (March), 32–39.
          The letters describe the early support Hayne rendered
       Lanier through encouragement and introductions. Lanier's
       criticism of Hayne's poetry as commonplace sentiments
       blended with diffuseness might have been more applicable to
       his own verse.

9   THOM, HELEN HOPKINS. Johns Hopkins: A Silhouette. Baltimore,
       Maryland: Johns Hopkins University Press, p. 79.
          Fits Lanier into the context of the founding of Johns
       Hopkins University.

10 WARD, WILLIAM HAYES. "Memorial," in The Poems of Sidney
       Lanier. Edited by Mary Day Lanier. New York: Scribner's,
       pp. xi–xli.
          Reprint of 1884.B7.

1929

11   WHITE, EDWARD L. "Reminiscences of Sidney Lanier." Johns
     Hopkins Alumni Magazine (Baltimore, Maryland), XVII (June),
     329–331.
          Recalls having heard Lanier play the flute in 1877, and
     later at Johns Hopkins observed how Lanier's serene dignity
     easily mastered his students.

1930 A BOOKS

1   SPENCER, THOMAS E. Sidney Lanier: A Study in Personality.
     St. Louis, Missouri: Hadley Vocational School Printing
     Department, 51pp.
          In this biographical survey of Lanier's career, examines
     the dual roles Lanier played as Southerner and Nationalist.

1930 B SHORTER WRITINGS

1   GARLAND, HAMLIN. Roadside Meetings. New York: Macmillan,
     pp. 144–153.
          Like Whitman, Lanier was an "evolutionist." Revision of
     1929.B2.

2   JACOBS, THORNWELL. "Sidney Lanier," in The Oglethorpe Book of
     Georgia Verse. Oglethorpe, Georgia: Oglethorpe University
     Press, pp. 146–148.
          Facsimile of Lanier's B.A. diploma.

3   KUHL, E. P. "Sidney Lanier and Edward Spencer." Studies in
     Philology, XXVII (July), 462–476.
          Describes how journalist and playwright Spencer wrote to
     Lippincott's of his admiration for "The Marshes of Glynn."

4   PARRINGTON, VERNON. Main Currents in American Thought. Vol.
     III. New York: Harcourt Brace, pp. xiii, 56, 334.
          Lanier rejected "both the genteel tradition and the
     ideals of the rising middle class." Had a "pagan" nature-
     love.

5   PRATT, WALDO S. and CHARLES BOYD. Grove's Dictionary of Music
     and Musicians: American Supplement. New York: Macmillan,
     p. 268.
          Describes Lanier's flute playing, his Science of English
     Verse, and musical imagery in his poetry.

1931 A BOOKS - NONE

1931 B SHORTER WRITINGS

1 BLANKENSHIP, RUSSELL. <u>American Literature as an Expression of</u>
   <u>the National Mind</u>. New York: Henry Holt, pp. 430–432.
   Feels that Lanier was "the one poetic artist of the
   Gilded Age and one of the very few true poets of America"
   who "instinctively mistrusted reason and relied upon feeling." His deficiencies resulted from living in an unroman-
   tic age.

2 BOURGEOIS, YVES R. "Sidney Lanier et Le Goffic." <u>Revue</u>
   <u>Anglo-Americaine</u> (Paris), VIII (June), 431–432.
   Draws a parallel between "The Revenge of Hamish" and Le
   Goffic's 1912 "Le Marquis rouge," a story. Finds Lanier
   austere and Le Goffic melodramatic.

3 GRAHAM, PHILIP. "Lanier's Reading." <u>Studies in English</u>
   (Austin, Texas), XI:63–89.
   Describes the books which Lanier cites in his work or
   known to be in his library. Then deduces the impacts of
   English poetry, German Romanticism, science, religion, etc.

4 HUBBELL, JAY B. "A Commencement Address by Sidney Lanier."
   <u>American Literature</u>, II (January), 385–404.
   Describes Lanier's Oglethorpe valedictorian address.

5 LANZ, HENRY. <u>The Physical Basis of Rime</u>. Palo Alto,
   California: Stanford University Press, pp. 179–180.
   Brief analysis of <u>The Science of English Verse</u>.

6 MAYFIELD, JOHN S. "Lanier in Lastekas." <u>Southwest Review</u>,
   XVII (October), 20–38.
   Recounts Lanier's brief sojourn in Texas.

7 SQUIRES, W. H. T. "Sidney Lanier," in his <u>The Land of</u>
   <u>Decision</u>. Portsmouth, Virginia: Printcraft Press,
   pp. 104–121.
   Brief biography which notes the importance of Baltimore
   in Lanier's life.

8 STARKE, AUBREY. "William Dean Howells and Sidney Lanier."
   <u>American Literature</u>, III (March), 79–82.
   Reviews Lanier's difficulties with Howells, especially
   with regard to "Corn."

1931

9   WILLIAMS, STANLEY T. "Sidney Lanier," in <u>American Writers on</u>
     <u>American Literature</u>. Edited by John Macy. New York:
     Horace Liveright, pp. 327–341.
         His poetry seems "nebulous" to modern readers and shows
     "the complete absence of emotional control." Yet, "cut off
     by moral principles from half the themes which are the sta-
     ples of modern poets, he yet sweeps us along on wings of
     fire, transfigures, exalts." His poetry is an "orgy of del-
     icate bliss," well suited to his themes of music and nature.

1932 A BOOKS – NONE

1932 B SHORTER WRITINGS

1   CALVERTON, V. F. <u>The Liberation of American Literature</u>.
     New York: Scribner's, pp. 11, 128, 138–143.
         Suggests that although Lanier recognized the "cultural
     desolation" of the South, he was a firm part of its tradi-
     tions. Traces the "religious fervor" of his poems to the
     rise of the middle class after the Civil War. Comparison
     to Whitman reveals that while the South was only intellec-
     tually democratic, the North was democratic in its very
     soil.

2   DABNEY, VIRGINIUS. <u>Liberalism in the South</u>. Chapel Hill:
     University of North Carolina Press, pp. 220–222.
         Finds Lanier interested in realism and harmony, things
     which would be inspiring to other post-Civil War poets.

3   EDWARDS, HARRY S. "Lanier, The Artist," in <u>Southern</u>
     <u>Literature</u>. Edited by William T. Wynn. New York:
     Prentice-Hall, pp. 405–408, 479.
         Discovers that "proportion" is the irreducible element
     in Lanier's art, and for this reason a thorough knowledge
     of <u>The Science of English Verse</u> is essential to an under-
     standing of any of his poems. "A Ballad of Trees and the
     Master" is so perfectly proportioned no single word could
     be removed without damaging the total effect.

4   FAGIN, N. BYRILLION. "Lanier: Poet of the South Today."
     <u>Johns Hopkins Alumni Magazine</u>, XX (March), 232–241.
         Maintains that unlike Poe, Lanier was influenced by the
     physical, political, social and intellectual atmosphere of
     the South. Yet his national interests made him a man with-
     out a country. Finds his Southern life accounted for his
     striking images, but it also created his flaws--bookish
     mannerisms, sentimentality, and moral goodness. Revised:
     1936.B6.

5   GRAHAM, PHILIP. "Lanier and Science." <u>American Literature</u>,
      IV (November), 288-292.
          Argues that science produced Lanier's "thought-pattern,
      his conceptions of art, and his imagery: rubbing hard
      against his social and religious traditions it created the
      friction which brought the spark of life to his poetry."

6   _____. "James Woodrow, Calvinist and Evolutionist." <u>Sewanee</u>
      <u>Review</u>, XL (July), 307-315.
          Finds that this formative teacher of Lanier's "precipi-
      tated the science-and-religion controversy" more than any
      other American of his generation.

7   KING, GRACE. <u>Memories of a Southern Woman of Letters</u>.
      New York: Macmillan, pp. 111-112.
          Recounts a meeting with Lanier's sister at which Lanier's
      poetry was read. Asserts that in France Lanier is called
      "greater even than Edgar Allan Poe."

8   LEWISOHN, LUDWIG. <u>Expression in America</u>. New York: Harper
      and Brothers, pp. 88-89.
          Discovers that Lanier's poems have a "touch of imagina-
      tive energy that was rare in those flat days."

9   LOVELL, CAROLINE COUPER. <u>The Golden Isles of Georgia</u>.
      Boston: Little, Brown, p. 272.
          Recalls Lanier's first reading of "The Marshes of Glynn,"
      to Mr. and Mrs. James Couper.

<u>1933 A BOOKS</u>

1   STARKE, AUBREY. <u>Sidney Lanier: A Biographical and Critical</u>
      <u>Study</u>. Chapel Hill: University of North Carolina Press,
      525pp.
          Offers detailed interpretations of all of Lanier's work
      in the factual context of his life. Major thesis argues
      that Lanier was far more sensitive than generally thought
      to the development of the "New South." Draws upon Lanier's
      dialect poems and "The Symphony," as well as his later work
      in supporting his thesis. Lanier is thus a forerunner of
      the "Fugitive-Agrarian" writers. Like those writers, Lanier
      was sensitive to the ways in which materialistic society had
      replaced a "traditional" society, leaving man at the mercy
      of abstractions. Lanier's responsiveness to music and na-
      ture enabled him to provide alternatives to the emptiness
      of modern life. Provides copious notes and documentation,
      as well as an extensive bibliography. Reprinted: 1964.A2.

1933

1933 B SHORTER WRITINGS

1   ANDERSON, CHARLES R. Review of <u>Sidney Lanier</u>. <u>American Literature</u>, V (November), 275–279.

        Discovers Starke's biography so minutely detailed that "little need for further and future study" is necessary. In his passion to create an American hero with a message for a time of social unrest, Starke shows a "failure to exclude irrelevant details" and "hesitancy in evaluating his sources." Thus, Starke was "unable to free himself even for the purposes of scholarship of a love that will not let him go." <u>See</u> 1933.A1.

2   ANON. Review of <u>Sidney Lanier</u>. London <u>Times Literary Supplement</u>, no. 1647 (24 August), p. 559.

        Maintains that "it is impossible to read Mr. Starke's book without sharing something of his belief in his subject's genius...and his significance as a Southerner with a vision and a message." Although Starke is most concerned with the visionary Lanier, he knows that Lanier's musical interests kept him from the wide audience he sought. Commends Starke for clarifying Lanier's message, which in his later poems was often diffuse. <u>See</u> 1933.A1.

3   BIRSS, JOHN H. "A Humorous Quatrain by Lanier." <u>American Literature</u>, V (November), 270.

        This quatrain originally appeared as "A Weather Vane" in <u>The Dial of the Old North Church</u> (Boston) on December 10, 1877.

4   BOPES, CHARLES F. "A Lost Occasional Poem by Sidney Lanier." <u>American Literature</u>, V (November), 269.

        Lanier had written a birthday poem for a distant relative of the author. The poem had been retained only as a remembered fragment.

5   BRENNER, RICA. <u>Twelve American Poets Before 1900</u>. New York: Harcourt, Brace, pp. 296–320.

        Asks, "Did he transform his life into poetry?" Answers by examining the inter-relation of his life and his poetic craft.

6   FRENCH, JOHN C. "First Drafts of Lanier's Verse." <u>Modern Language Notes</u>, XLVIII (January), 27–31.

        Presents drafts of Lanier's "Individuality," "Marsh Song—At Sunset," and "Ode to the Johns Hopkins University." These variants were incorporated in 1945.B1.

1933

7   MALONE, KEMP. "Sidney Lanier." <u>Johns Hopkins Alumni</u>
    <u>Magazine</u> (Baltimore), XXI (March), 244-249.
        Though a poet he made brilliant scientific generaliza-
    tions in his criticism of the evolution of the novel and in
    "experimental phonetics." The "core of Lanier the man of
    science" rested in his eagerness to "plumb the secret
    springs of his art."

8   MIMS, EDWIN. "Sidney Lanier." <u>Dictionary of American</u>
    <u>Biography</u>. Vol. X. New York: Scribner's, pp. 601-605.
    Condenses his remarks of 1905.A1.

9   REDE, KENNETH. "The Sidney Lanier Memorial Alcove." <u>American</u>
    <u>Book Collector</u> (Baltimore), III (May-June), 301-304.
        Recounts Lanier's Maryland contacts, from his imprison-
    ment in Point Lookout during the Civil War, to his teaching
    at Johns Hopkins University. Explains that the "Alcove"
    was created at Johns Hopkins to house Lanier's memorabilia,
    editions of his work, criticism about him, etc. in 1925.

10 SHUSTER, GEORGE N. "Idealist." <u>Commonweal</u>, XVIII (16 June),
    192-193.
        Review of <u>Sidney Lanier</u> 1933.A1. Finds that Starke makes
    Lanier seem "genuinely manly and interesting," but that
    Lanier's poetry has "less need for apology than he supplies."

11 STARKE, AUBREY. "Sidney Lanier: Man of Science in the Field
    of Letters." <u>American Scholar</u>, II (October), 289-297.
        Asserts in his general survey that there is "no essential
    difference" between the poetry written before and after
    Lanier's theories of verse were formulated.

12 _____. "Lanier's Appreciation of Whitman." <u>American Scholar</u>,
    II (October), 398-408.
        Recounts the mistaken view of Lanier's attitude toward
    Whitman resulting from censorship of his views in <u>The Eng-</u>
    <u>lish Novel</u>. Collating texts, Starke restores Lanier's ideas
    and finds his evaluation "one of the clearest and most
    just...one of the bravest and boldest" yet made.

13 _____. "More about Lanier." <u>New Republic</u>, LXXVI (1 November),
    337-338.
        A reply to the negative reaction of Allen Tate to his
    biography. Speaking for Southern writers, Tate had rejected
    Starke's view that Lanier was their precursor. Starke
    vigorously objects.

14 TATE, ALLEN. "A Southern Romantic." <u>New Republic</u>, LXXVI
    (30 August), 67-70.

1933

Objects to Starke's view that Lanier was a precursor of
modern Southern writers or the "New South." Insists that
Lanier failed as a poet and provided only a confused anti-
Southern and self-serving propaganda for Northern industri-
alism. For support, Tate refers primarily to Lanier's "The
Psalm of the West" and "The Centennial Cantata."

15 _____. "More About Lanier." New Republic, LXXVI (1 November),
338.
A reply to Starke's response to his review. See
1933.B13 and B14.

16 WANN, LOUIS. The Rise of Realism. New York: Macmillan,
pp. 770–772.
Detailed bibliography as well as notes to several poems,
including an 1876 review of "The Centennial Cantata." See
1876.B2–B3.

17 WARREN, ROBERT PENN. "The Blind Poet: Sidney Lanier."
American Review, II (November), 27–45.
Compares Lanier's poetry unfavorably to that of various
Jacobean poets. Concludes that Lanier could not write poems
with coherent images because he never truly "saw" any of
the world.

1934 A BOOKS - NONE

1934 B SHORTER WRITINGS

1 CHRISTY, ARTHUR. "The Orientalism of Sidney Lanier." Aryan
Path (Bombay, India), V (October), 638–641.
Essentially treats "Nirvana."

2 OLNEY, CLARK. "Archaisms in the Poetry of Sidney Lanier."
Notes and Queries (London), CLXVI (28 April), 292–294.
Lists varieties of antique diction and archaic verbal
forms in Lanier's poetry.

3 RANSOM, JOHN CROWE. "Hearts and Heads." American Review, II
(March), 554–571.
Mediates the positions of Aubrey Starke and Allen Tate
concerning Starke's biography of Lanier. Finds Lanier un-
acceptable as a precursor and unimportant as a poet because
he is not in the "tradition" of "metaphysical" poetry.

4 STARKE, AUBREY. "The Agrarians Deny a Leader." American
Review, II (March), 534–553.

Defends Lanier against Allen Tate and others, while insisting that Lanier's sensitivity to the meaning of agrari-
anism to every aspect of American life makes him the nineteenth century forerunner of the "Fugitive-Agrarians."

5 _____. "An Omnibus of Poets." Colophon (New York), IV
(March), Part 16, 12pp. [unnumbered].
Concerns A Masque of Poets to which Lanier contributed
"The Marshes of Glynn."

6 _____. "Sidney Lanier as a Musician." Musical Quarterly
(New York), XX (October), 384–400.
Reviews Lanier's contact with musical New York and Baltimore when he played the flute there for major orchestras
and private groups.

1935 A BOOKS

1 LORENZ, LINCOLN. The Life of Sidney Lanier. New York:
Coward and McCann, 313pp.
Emphasizes anecdote and hearsay.

1935 B SHORTER WRITINGS

1 ALLEN, GAY WILSON. American Prosody. New York: American
Book, pp. 277–306.
Provides a detailed and analytical investigation of the
prosodic complexity of Lanier's poetry, particularly the
later work.

2 JACKSON, LENA E. and AUBREY STARKE. "New Light on the
Ancestry of Sidney Lanier." Virginia Magazine of History
and Biography (Richmond, Virginia), XLIII (April), 160–168.
Establishes Lanier's descent from John Lanier who parti-
cipated in Bacon's Rebellion, 1676, and died in Virginia in
1719. Offering a review of Lanier's interest in geneology
and providing a careful documentation of his relations, the
authors hope that some day it will be firmly proven that
Lanier was descended from musicians of the court of Queen
Elizabeth.

3 LAMAR, E. DOLLY BLOUNT. "Nominating Sidney Lanier for the
Hall of Fame." Saturday Review of Literature, XII
(31 August), 9.
Describes the "Brief" she helped to prepare to the Elec-
tors of the Hall of Fame. The "Brief" contained memorials

1935

and critical opinions by various commentators including
H. L. Mencken.

4   MAYFIELD, JOHN S. "Sidney Lanier's Immoral Bird." American
Book Collector (Baltimore), VI (June), 200–203.
Suggests that Bayard Taylor's "Studies in Animal Nature"
may have influenced Lanier's previously unpublished 1877
poem "An Immoral Bird," concerning a turkey.

1936 A BOOKS

1   BEESON, LEOLA. Sidney Lanier at Oglethorpe University.
Macon, Georgia: J. W. Burke, 61pp.
Beeson describes several debates in which Lanier took
part, basing her study on "the Minutes of the Thalian Society" for 1859–1861.

1936 B SHORTER WRITINGS

1   ADAMS, RANDOLPH. "Notes and Queries: Correction by Lanier."
Colophon (New York), II (Autumn), 132.
A minor correction by Lanier was not included in the
1884 edition of his poems.

2   ANDERSON, CHARLES R. Review of Lorenz's Life of Sidney
Lanier. American Literature, VIII (May), 232–233.
Confirms his opinion that Starke's biography of Lanier
is definitive. Lorenz "fails to add a shred of significant
new material" in this "popular" biography, though he, unlike Starke, had access to private papers and letters.

3   BENÉT, WILLIAM ROSE. Review of Lorenz's Life of Sidney
Lanier. Saturday Review of Literature, XIII (25 January),
18.
This biography made a strong "masculine" poet seem fuzzy.

4   BOYNTON, PERCY. Literature and American Life. Boston: Ginn
and Company, pp. 577–585.
Asserts that Lanier was "intensely local but unpartisan."
He responded to the insistent call for a Southern literature
in the 1870's.

5   CLARK, HARRY HAYDEN. Major American Poets. New York:
American Book, pp. 903–913.
Finds "etherealization" essential to Lanier's thought.
Contributes extensive, documented notes on Lanier's poetry
and prose, with annotated checklist.

1936

6   FAGIN, N. BYRILLION. "Sidney Lanier: Poet of the South."
     Poet Lore (Philadelphia), XLIII:161-168.
          Though distinctly Southern, Lanier is more than Southern
     in appeal: "his poems are often greater than their...moral
     purpose." Essentially a realist, the Southern environment
     enforced his sentimentalism. Revision of 1932.B4.

7   HARRISON, JOHN M. and AUBREY STARKE. "Maternal Ancestors of
     Sidney Lanier." Virginia Magazine of History and Biography
     (Richmond, Virginia), XLIV (January), 73-80.
          Although Lanier insisted that his musical sensitivity was
     inherited from his paternal ancestors, Harrison contends
     that his poetic talent was inherited from his maternal an-
     cestors, who were men and women of integrity, bravery, some
     wealth and social position, but neither poets nor musicians.

8   _____. "Maternal Ancestors of Sidney Lanier." Virginia
     Magazine of History and Biography (Richmond, Virginia),
     XLIV (April), 160-174.
          Continuation of 1936.B7. Reveals that Lanier's maternal
     line may be traced to the 1500's and to John Jenners, owner
     of Aston Hall which Washington Irving used as "Bracebridge
     Hall."

9   HARTWICK, HARRY. "Bibliography," in A History of American
     Letters. Edited by Walter F. Taylor. Boston: American
     Book, pp. 550-553.
          An extensive bibliography of secondary works.

10   HUBBELL, JAY B. "Sidney Lanier," in his American Life in
     Literature. Vol. III. New York: Harper's, pp. 209-228.
          Asserts in this headnote to eleven poems and selected
     letters that Lanier was the most important poet to emerge
     between the Civil War and 1900. Provides expanded notes to
     "The Marshes of Glynn" and "The Revenge of Hamish."

11   JACKSON, LENA E. "Sidney Lanier in Florida." Florida
     Historical Society Quarterly, XV (October), 118-124.
          Describes Lanier's visits to Florida 1875-1877 and the
     eleven poems written about Florida or planned there, parti-
     cularly "A Florida Sunday," and "Tampa Robbins."

12   PARKS, EDD WINFIELD. Southern Poets. New York: American
     Book, pp. lxix-lxxvii, cxiii-cxix, 170-201.
          Suggests that Lanier's philosophical-critical views and
     his musical prosody experiments never fused because he
     wanted to flee from the ailing South. His main failure con-
     sisted in the substitution of vague sensibilities for real
     thought.

1936

13 STARKE, AUBREY. "An Uncollected Sonnet by Sidney Lanier."
    American Literature, VII (January), 460–463.
        Surmises that an anonymous sonnet found in the Southern
    Literary Messenger (1862) might be Lanier's.

14 ____. "Annulet Andrews: Poet." South Atlantic Quarterly,
    XXXV (April), 194–200.
        Andrews's poem to Lanier in 1887 adapted "old forms to
    new patterns," showing she comprehended his practice and
    precept.

15 TAYLOR, WALTER F. A History of American Letters. Boston:
    American Book, pp. 277–281.
        Asserts that Lanier equaled Tennyson as a poet of na-
    ture. Reprinted in 1956.B6.

16 VOIGT, G. P. "Sidney Lanier." Saturday Review of Literature,
    XIII (4 April), 9.
        Calling Lanier a "lady-like Professor" ignores his
    struggles with illness, poverty, injustice, and oppression.

1937 A BOOKS – NONE

1937 B SHORTER WRITINGS

1   BUCK, PAUL HERMAN. The Road to Reunion, 1865–1900. Boston:
    Little, Brown, pp. 227–228.
        Lanier felt the South integral to the nation.

2   GRAHAM, PHILIP. "A Note on Lanier's Music." Studies in
    English (Austin, Texas), XVII:107–111.
        Suggests that Lanier "probably borrowed the musical pat-
    tern" of "The Song of the Chattahoochee" from Coleridge's
    "Song by Glycine."

3   ROQUIE, MARGARET B. "Sidney Lanier, Poet-Musician." Etude
    (Philadelphia), LV (September), 576, 617.

1938 A BOOKS – NONE

1938 B SHORTER WRITINGS

1   ALLEN, GAY WILSON. "Sidney Lanier as a Literary Critic."
    Philological Quarterly, XVII (April), 121–138.
        Lanier had "more grip" on the literary problems of his
    day than Lowell, Emerson, or Whitman. He deserves credit
    for bringing science "to the aid of literary criticism."

2   HOBEIKA, JOHN E. "Sidney Lanier." The Southern Magazine, IV
     (May), 16-17, 37.

3   MELTON, WIGHTMAN F. Poems of Trees: A Sidney Lanier Memorial.
     Vol. VII. Atlanta, Georgia: Curtis, pp. 7-17.
        This series, begun in 1932, contains poems and essays
     pertinent to Lanier's concerns. This volume includes the
     work of a great many writers, almost entirely about trees.
     It also contains excerpts about trees from Lanier's work.
     Additionally: four essays concern Lanier: Judge Lucien P.
     Goodrich's "Sidney Clopton Lanier, of Griffin, Georgia"
     suggests the source of Lanier's middle name; John C. French's
     "Sidney Lanier and Johns Hopkins University" considers
     Lanier's scholarly ambitions and reviews the memorials given
     him; the anonymous "Sidney Lanier Memorials" describes
     memorials throughout the country; and Ruby Richardson Wal-
     ton's "Sidney Lanier--The Poet-Musician" provides a tribute
     to his dual talents.

4   MOTT, FRANK LUTHER. A History of American Magazines.
     Cambridge, Massachusetts: Harvard University Press,
     passim.
        Contains various facts related to publications accepting
     Lanier's work.

5   PARKS, EDD WINFIELD. Segments of Southern Thought. Athens:
     University of Georgia Press, pp. 62-69, 104-110.
        Argues that Lanier never fused his philosophical and
     prosodic interests. Instead, his many interests "drew his
     mind hither and yon." On the other hand, since the South
     couldn't support an artist of his type, Lanier's natural
     pictorial gifts were frustrated; otherwise, he might have
     developed as a local colorist. In attempting to be a
     philosophical poet, Lanier fell into "honeyed abstractions,"
     but in the late marsh poems he succeeded as a "poet of
     feeling."

1939 A BOOKS - NONE

1939 B SHORTER WRITINGS

1   EMERSON, DOROTHY. "Sidney Lanier, the Bread and the Flute."
     Scholastic, XXXIV (4 February), 27-E.
        Brief biographical notes.

2   GRAHAM, PHILIP and JOSEPH JONES. A Concordance to the Poems
     of Sidney Lanier. Austin: University of Texas Press,
     447pp.

1939

Alphabetical list of every word used by Lanier in the
editions of his poetry and the 1929 Poem Outlines, along
with some uncollected works. Reprinted: 1969.B3.

3   KELLY, FREDERICK. "Sidney Lanier at the Peabody Institute."
    Peabody Bulletin (Baltimore, Maryland), (December),
    pp. 35–38.
    Examines the letters for evidence of Lanier's interest
    in music, especially musical theory, while in Baltimore.

4   LONG, FRANCIS TAYLOR. "The Life of Richard Malcolm Johnston
    in Maryland, 1867–1898." Maryland Historical Magazine
    (Baltimore, Maryland), XXXIV (December), 305–324.
    Lanier offered this fellow Georgian, who also lived in
    Baltimore, criticism which helped him publish his first
    novel.

5   MELTON, WIGHTMAN F. Poems of Trees: A Sidney Lanier Memorial.
    Vol. VIII. Atlanta, Georgia: Curtis, pp. 8–18.
    Contains a great many poems concerning Lanier and his
    nature subjects, as well as four brief essays related to
    him. Dewing Woodward's "Sidney Lanier—a Reminiscence" re-
    counts how Woodward attended one of Lanier's courses at
    Johns Hopkins in which Lanier played the violin. Aline B.
    Carter's "Sidney Lanier in San Antonio" describes the con-
    nections Lanier made with musical San Antonio. Captain
    John Saulsbury Short's "Sidney Lanier, Poet-Musician," at-
    tempts to show how he developed "symphonies" in his poetry.
    The anonymous "Sidney Lanier Triumphant" recounts how
    Lanier played his flute among the birds.

6   MILES, J. TOM. "Nineteenth Century Southern Literature and
    Its Five Greatest Poets." Southern Literary Messenger, I
    (September), 599.
    This brief sketch links Lanier to Timrod and Hayne among
    others, and contends that his moral purpose helped him re-
    sist "art-for-art's-sake" doctrines.

7   RYAN, W. CARSON. "The Johns Hopkins: University Pioneer."
    Studies in Early Graduate Education, no. 30. New York:
    Carnegie Foundation, pp. 15–46.
    Recounts how a student recalled that Lanier exemplified
    "the tragedy of his life" in his body's feebleness "that
    would not allow him to stand in delivering his lectures."

8   WOOD, CLEMENT. "The Influence of Poe and Lanier on Modern
    Literature." Southern Literary Messenger (Richmond,
    Virginia), I (April), 237–40.

Contends that both Poe and Lanier were not romantics, since both confronted life directly or symbolically, rather than "sugar-coating" "life's actual desires." Thus, both poets anticipate modern realism.

9   _____. "Lanier's Religion was Unorthodox." Southern Literary Messenger (Richmond, Virginia), I (September), 641.
Replies to criticism of his view that Lanier found no solution in religion.

1940 A BOOKS

1   ANON. Sidney Lanier. Baltimore, Maryland: Johns Hopkins University Press, unpaginated.
This program of the meeting of February 3, 1940, at the Peabody Institute commemorates Lanier with remarks by Dr. John C. French, Governor Herbert R. O'Connor, Isaiah Bowman, and descriptions of music by and about Lanier played on this occasion. Bowman's "Remembering the Beauty" focuses on the truthful reportage of Lanier's Florida.

2   JONES, MARY CALLAWAY. Sidney Lanier: A Chronological Record of Authenticated Facts. Macon, Georgia: privately published, 5pp.
Lists Lanier's dates and activities, with notes and sources.

1940 B SHORTER WRITINGS

1   ANDERSON, CHARLES R. "Charles Gayarré and Paul Hayne: The Last Literary Cavaliers," in American Studies in Honor of William Kenneth Boyd. Edited by David K. Jackson. Durham, North Carolina: Duke University Press, pp. 255–256.
Records that Hayne generously sponsored Lanier's career until Lanier's national recognition left Hayne "bewildered to see himself so quickly eclipsed." Hayne came to doubt Lanier's Old South loyalty.

2   ANON. "Significant Dates in Sidney Lanier's Life." Southern Literary Messenger, II (January), 12.
Provides a brief chronology of important dates.

3   BILLING, BEATRICE. "On Wings of Song." Southern Literary Messenger, II (January), 13–18.
Three constants in Lanier's life were his courage, valor, and dedication to music. They combined to produce the

1940

fearlessly individual "Marshes of Glynn," America's greatest poem.

4   BLAIR, GORDON. <u>Father Tabb</u>. Richmond, Virginia: Whittet and Shepperson, pp. 55–65.
      Includes comments on Lanier's reverential letters to Tabb.

5   HANKINS, J. DeWITT. "Unpublished Letters of Sidney Lanier." <u>Southern Literary Messenger</u> (Richmond, Virginia), II (January), 5–11.
      These letters to Virginia Hankins 1862–1880 contain comments about literature and love. Through extracts from his poems and his favorite poets, Lanier stresses the need for new forms.

6   MAGRUDER, MARY LANIER. "The Laniers." <u>Southern Literary Messenger</u> (Richmond, Virginia), II (January), 26–27.
      Concerns Lanier's ancestors and descendants.

7   ORIANS, G. HARRISON. <u>A Short History of American Literature</u>. New York: F. S. Crofts, pp. 196–197.
      Contends that Lanier was "essentially a poet of unfulfilled promise."

8   ORR, OLIVER. "Sidney Lanier's Fame and Memorials." <u>Southern Literary Messenger</u> (Richmond, Virginia), II (January), 28–32.
      Records various memorials and monuments in Georgia, Florida, Alabama, Texas, Oklahoma, North Carolina, South Carolina, Maryland, Pennsylvania, and California.

9   SHACKFORD, J. ATKINS. "Sidney Lanier as a Southerner." <u>Sewanee Review</u>, XLVIII (April), 153–173.
      Challenges the view of Robert Penn Warren, Allen Tate and John Crowe Ransom that Lanier "had little to say to this century in substance or technique." Lanier did not temper his ideas to public opinion, nor did he flee the South in going to Baltimore. His dialect poems encouraged subsistence farming. Directs attention to Tate's misreadings of Lanier's work. <u>See</u> 1940.B10, B11.

10 _____. "Sidney Lanier as a Southerner." <u>Sewanee Review</u>, XLVIII (July), 348–355.
      <u>See</u> 1940.B9.

11 _____. "Sidney Lanier as a Southerner." <u>Sewanee Review</u>, XLVIII (October), 480–493.
      <u>See</u> 1940.B9.

12   SHORT, JOHN SAULSBURY. "Sidney Lanier 'Familiar Citizen of the Town.'" <u>Maryland Historical Magazine</u> (Baltimore, Maryland), XXXV (June), 121–146.
     Dividing Lanier's career into the Georgia and Maryland decades, provides a detailed survey of his Baltimore literary and musical experiences.

1941 A BOOKS

1   ABERNETHY, CECIL. "A Critical Edition of Sidney Lanier's <u>Tiger Lilies</u>." Ph.D. Dissertation, Vanderbilt University.
     Provides a detailed analysis of the historical context of the novel as well as extensive notes. This work formed the basis of the Centennial Edition of <u>Tiger-Lilies</u>. See 1945.B6.

2   COULSON, EDWIN R. and RICHARD WEBB. <u>Sidney Lanier Poet and Prosodist</u>. Atlanta: University of Georgia Press, 103pp.
     Although this is a unified study of Lanier, it contains two essays written thirty-eight years apart: Richard Webb's "Sidney Lanier, Poet and Prosodist" and Edwin R. Coulson's "Lanier's Place as American Poet and Prosodist." Webb's essay, written in 1903, identifies Lanier as "an idealist of the highest type," saved from provincialism by his great ideas. "Hebrew" in his moral earnestness, he is "Greek" in his love of beauty. However, Lanier's execution fails to meet his ideal because of his circumstances, his "failure to restrict at all times his extremely active imagination," and his theory of verse. Thus it is mistaken to compare Lanier to Tennyson since he never had Tennyson's situation in which to work. In addition, his many interests kept him from perfecting any of them. Furthermore, <u>The Science of English Verse</u> committed him to a straining for musical effects which become artificial, aggravating weaknesses already in his poetry. Still, Lanier had "one of the truest and richest nature-notes in American poetry."
     In "Lanier's Place as American Poet and Prosodist," Edwin R. Coulson updates Webb's evaluation. He attempts to assess Lanier's influence by codifying the results of queries he had put to practicing poets like Conrad Aiken, and by considering the indebtedness of present-day theories of prosody to Lanier. He concludes that he had individual impact upon specific poets and prosodists but developed no "school" in either.

1941

1941 B SHORTER WRITINGS

1   ANON. "Poetry Corner." <u>Scholastic</u>, XXXVIII (28 April), 20.
Provides a general introduction to Lanier's major poems.

2   CARGILL, OSCAR. <u>Intellectual America</u>. New York: Macmillan,
pp. 520, 734.
Places Lanier among poets and others striving to teach
literature "scientifically," though <u>The Science of English
Verse</u> was hardly the start of a science of literature.

3   CASH, W. J. <u>The Mind of the South</u>. New York: Random House,
p. 145.
Sees Lanier as "authentically a poet as any other American of his time, Walt Whitman alone excepted," though he
was "both derivative and didactic."

4   HOLLAR, ROSITA H. "Lanier, Agrarian Poet-Prophet." <u>Southern
Literary Messenger</u> (Richmond, Virginia), III (February),
71–73.
For his dedication to the idea of "diversification" in
farming and his tribute to Southern soil in "Corn," Lanier
could take the "4-H" pledge of Head, Hand, Heart and Health.

5   KELLY, FREDERICK. "Lanier's House on Denmead Street."
<u>Maryland Historical Magazine</u> (Baltimore, Maryland), XXXVI
(June), 231–232.
Discovered that Denmead Street changed position in Mary-
land counties and so was not listed in old Baltimore street
directories. Lanier's home, 33 Denmead Street, became 20
E. 20th Street, and was later demolished.

6   KLEMM, GUSTAV. "Sidney Lanier: Poet, Man and Musician."
<u>Etude</u> (Philadelphia), LIX (May), 299–300, 342.

1942 A BOOKS - NONE

1942 B SHORTER WRITINGS

1   DOYLE, SISTER TERESA ANN, O.S.B. "The Indomitable Courage of
Sidney Lanier." <u>Catholic World</u> (New York), CLVI (December),
293–301.
Lanier's centenary in this time of war recalls that his
courage was rooted in love of mankind, patriotism, and social consciousness—creators of a manhood equal to the
Fascists.

2   OEHSER, PAUL H.   "Sidney Lanier, Nature Poet."   Nature
    Magazine (Washington), XXXV (November), 468, 500.
        Identifies topographical features and natural life of
    interest to Lanier.

3   POPE, JOHN C.   The Rhythm of Beowulf.   New Haven, Connecticut:
    Yale University Press, pp. vii–viii.
        Admits that he was inspired by Lanier's recognition that
    "rhythm depends on the temporal relations of accents" in
    his study of Beowulf.

1943 A BOOKS – NONE

1943 B SHORTER WRITINGS

1   MOORE, ELIZABETH HALEY.   "Sidney Lanier."   Alabama Historical
    Quarterly (Montgomery), V (Spring), 35–46.
        Survey and biographical introduction to his life by the
    Daughters of the American Revolution.

2   SUTRO, OTTILIE.   "The Wednesday Club: A Brief Sketch from
    Authentic Sources."   Maryland Historical Magazine
    (Baltimore), XXXVIII (March), 60–68.
        Lanier belonged to the "Wednesday Club" of Baltimore,
    devoted to music and amateur theatricals.

1944 A BOOKS – NONE

1944 B SHORTER WRITINGS

1   ANDERSON, CHARLES R.   The American Philosophical Society Year
    Book.   Philadelphia: American Philosophical Society,
    pp. 234–238.
        Summarizes the progress of "The Centennial Edition of
    the Works of Sidney Lanier," partly sponsored by the Ameri-
    can Philosophical Society.   Describes the necessity for
    this edition and cites the "chaotic state of the materials"
    hampering progress.   Details the methods of editorship
    governing each volume.

2   JONES, WEIMAR.   "Sidney Lanier's Visits to Old Asheville
    Citizen Recalled."   Asheville Citizen-Times (Asheville,
    North Carolina), (27 February), Section A, p. 11.
        Conveys the impression of several of the citizenry about
    Lanier's health visits and identifies local landmarks asso-
    ciated with him.

1944

3   ROSEBERY, MARGUERITE T. "Sidney Lanier, Poet of Democracy."
      <u>Southern Literary Messenger</u>, VI:195-199.
         To promote his entrance into the "Hall of Fame," she
      reviews his denunciations of economic tyranny.

1945 A BOOKS - NONE

1945 B SHORTER WRITINGS

1   ANDERSON, CHARLES R. "General Preface" and "Introduction," in
      <u>The Centennial Edition of the Works of Sidney Lanier</u>.
      Vol. I. Edited by the author. Baltimore, Maryland:
      Johns Hopkins University Press, pp. v-xiii, xxi-xc, 286-385.
         The "Introduction" shows that understanding of Lanier's
      work demands knowledge of his life. Stresses his divided
      interests as well as the deleterious situation in which he
      wrote. Anderson asserts that Lanier needed "felt experi-
      ences" for his best poems. Crucial were the impact of Emer-
      son and Whitman. His concern for science as well as the
      development of his personal spirituality were significant
      forces in his maturity, while Lanier's interest in blending
      music to poetry, like his sensitivity to social problems,
      looked forward to later developments in poetry. Anderson
      includes estimates of various critics at the time of
      Lanier's death. Highly detailed and voluminous notes with
      all variants of the poems are appended to this volume.
         In his "General Preface" Anderson describes the diffi-
      culties of creating the "Centennial Edition." It consti-
      tutes the first time Lanier's works have been issued as a
      set, and the works are in "definitive form."

2   _____ and AUBREY H. STARKE. "Introduction," in <u>The Centennial
      Edition of the Works of Sidney Lanier</u>. Vol. VII.
      Baltimore, Maryland: Johns Hopkins University Press,
      pp. vii-lxiii.
         In this introduction to their edition of Lanier's letters
      (composing Volumes VII-X of the <u>Centennial Edition</u>) Anderson
      and Starke assert that Lanier revealed himself "with unusual
      candor," thus making a "remarkably full" autobiographical
      record. Of 1597 letters by Lanier, 1161 are represented,
      of which 274 were previously published. The editors provide
      a calendar in Volume X, revaling an almost daily record of
      letters. The editors' purpose is to fill in the musical,
      literary and scholarly background not found in the letters,
      and they limit their study to the last eight years of
      Lanier's life, since only then did he give himself com-
      pletely to the artistic life. They trace Lanier's musical

life in Baltimore, noting his gradual emergence as a vir-
tuoso and respected composer, though composition of music
ceased in 1874 when he turned his attention more deliberately to poetry. Though Baltimore was not a literary hub,
Lanier made important artistic contacts in the "Wednesday
Club." The editors then examine his attempt to secure an
academic position at Johns Hopkins and chart his voluminous
reading in the late 1870's. His marginalia reveal linguis-
tic and prosodic interests. See 1894.B8, B9.

3   BAUM, PAULL FRANKLIN. "Introduction," in The Centennial
Edition of the Works of Sidney Lanier. Vol. II.
Baltimore, Maryland: Johns Hopkins University Press,
pp. vii–xlviii.
     In this introduction to his edition of The Science of
English Verse and ten essays on music, Baum provides a
scholarly analysis of the composition and significance of
these works. He approaches them with a fund of historical
detail. Baum includes a comparison of the various drafts
of The Science of English Verse with detailed descriptions
of Lanier's various lectures on prosody and essays developed
from them "to illustrate the growth of his ideas on prosody."
Baum makes a careful evaluation of the influences of his
theories on other writers, while comparing them to other
theories. Although Baum cites Lanier as "the first student
of the phenomenon of English verse to start with an analysis
of the acoustic values of words," he criticizes some of his
contentions, especially his assertion that "English syl-
lables are exactly equal in time" to one another. In four
remaining pages Baum describes ten essays on music in which
Lanier argues his theories with other writers, praises German music, and examines the place of music in man's moral
life.

4   GRAHAM, PHILIP. "Introduction," in The Centennial Edition of
the Works of Sidney Lanier. Vol. VI. Baltimore, Maryland:
Johns Hopkins University Press, pp. vii–xxv.
     Graham establishes the background of Lanier's journalism,
especially detailing his plans to write a history of Texas.
But conditions demanded that he write pot-boilers, so he
stayed closer to home and composed another travel book,
Florida. Graham analyzes his use of his sources. The editor concludes that writing these pot-boilers, necessitated
by his diseased lungs, "curtailed the boldness of his
thought."

5   _____ and FRIEDA THIES. "Bibliography," in The Centennial
Edition of the Works of Sidney Lanier. Vol. VI. Baltimore,
Maryland: Johns Hopkins University Press, pp. 379–412.

1945

In this unannotated bibliography of his work and writing
about him, the compilers have included many items from
Southern newspapers in their determination to be exhaustive.

6 GREEVER, GARLAND and CECIL ABERNETHY. "Introduction," in The
Centennial Edition of the Works of Sidney Lanier. Vol. V.
Baltimore, Maryland: Johns Hopkins University Press,
pp. vii-lx.
In this introduction to an edition of Tiger-Lilies and
fourteen essays mainly from the 1870's, Greever acknowledges
important debts to the critical edition of his novel made by
Cecil Abernethy, but takes full responsibility for the introduction; thus, it shall be viewed as his work. Greever
identifies Tiger-Lilies as "a first book fairly a-bristle
with the ideas which the author was to amplify and expound
through the rest of his life." Only "Nature" by Emerson
is similar in this regard. Greever explicates the title
as a dualism of ethereal and selfish love, and he connects
the novel to German Romance, compares it to other war
novels, traces biographical allusions, and explores its
local color as a clue to the work as a transition between
Romanticism and Realism. He also analyzes the manuscript.
Greever charts the significance of the essays, particularly
"Paul H. Hayne," "Retrospects and Prospects," and "Nature-
Metaphors" as examples of Lanier's hatred of materialism
and inclination toward the theory of etherealization. In
"The New South" Greever detects a frank but warm appraisal
of the South from a scientific-historical-poetic perspec-
tive. See 1941.A1.

7 McKEITHAN, DANIEL. A Collection of Hayne Letters. Austin:
University of Texas Press, pp. 460-461.
In an 1879 letter from Paul H. Hayne to John G. James,
Hayne records his agreement that Lanier was wrong in accusing Hayne's poetry of "straining after effect" since that
was Lanier's own problem. James later replied with a criticism of Lanier's poem on Bayard Taylor, accusing it of being
less "natural" than one by Hayne on the same subject.

8 MALONE, KEMP. "Introduction," in The Centennial Edition of
the Works of Sidney Lanier. Vol. III. Edited by the
author. Baltimore, Maryland: Johns Hopkins University
Press, pp. vii-xxiv.
Examines two sets of lectures on Shakespeare and prints
these separately, tracing the place of each lecture in
Lanier's plan. Provides a detailed analysis of his prepara-
tion for a series of adult classes. Since he was concerned
with "forerunners" of Shakespeare, Lanier's interest in Old

English and Middle English literature are charted. Malone concludes: "Given the health and strength to go on, he would surely have mastered the philological discipline and might well have become one of the leading Anglicists of his day."

9 _____ and CLARENCE GOHDES. "Introduction," in The Centennial Edition of the Works of Sidney Lanier. Vol. IV. Edited by the authors. Baltimore, Maryland: Johns Hopkins University Press, pp. vii–xi.
   Trace the development of Lanier's work on the English novel through his 1881 Johns Hopkins lectures. Lanier's view of Whitman is considered against the views of the academic world in which he wrote. Indicate that he was "one of our first critics to project a lengthy application" of the psychology of personality to the history of literature.

10 MELCHER, F. G. "Authors to the Hall of Fame." Publisher's Weekly, CXLVIII (10 November), 2127.
   Notes Lanier preceded Thoreau into the Hall of Fame.

11 MIMS, EDWIN. Great Writers as Interpretors of Religion. New York: Abingdon-Cokesbury Press, pp. 128–130.
   Contends that in his marsh poems Lanier transfigured the ugly marshes and attained "the furthest reach of nineteenth century romanticism or idealism."

1946 A BOOKS - NONE

1946 B SHORTER WRITINGS

1 ANON. "Shadowed Lives." Scholastic, XLVIII (25 March), 22.
   A brief biography emphasizing Lanier's heroism.

2 ANON. Review of The Centennial Edition of the Works of Sidney Lanier. United States Quarterly Booklet, II (September), 172–173.
   Calls this edition an "unparalleled quarry for future investigators."

3 CHEW, S. C. "Lanier in Retrospect." Christian Science Monitor (10 August), p. 12.
   Review of The Centennial Edition of the Works of Sidney Lanier. The "so modern professional scholarship" is a strange contrast to the "old-fashioned tone" of the writings, which are of only historical value.

1946

4   COMMAGER, HENRY STEELE. "'A Gallant and Heroic Figure.'"
    New York Times Book Review (20 October), pp. 6, 38, 40.
        Review of The Centennial Edition of the Works of Sidney
    Lanier. Details the contents and intentions of each volume
    of Lanier's collected works, concluding that while his life
    is of importance to modern readers, his poetry is destined
    to survive only in anthology pieces.

5   HARRISON, JAMES G. "Sidney Lanier as a Man of Letters."
    Transactions of the Huguenot Society of South Carolina,
    no. 51, pp. 25–32.
        Maintains that Lanier showed signs of his French ancestry
    in his musical involvements.

6   HUBBELL, JAY B. Review of The Centennial Edition of the Works
    of Sidney Lanier. American Literature, XVIII (November),
    254–256.
        Describes this work as "an important event in the history
    of American scholarship" since it is the first work by a
    major writer to be fully, competently edited.

7   TODD, AUBREY. Review of Sidney Lanier: Poet and Prosodist.
    Southern Packet, II (April), 3.
        Contends that this is the "first attempt to give an
    honest and intelligent appraisal of the man and his works
    as viewed by the present generation."

8   WHICHER, GEORGE F. "Sidney Lanier's Letters." Forum, CVI
    (October), 354–358.
        Finds The Science of English Verse alone of all Lanier's
    works can be read for its own merit, though the dialect
    poems contain surprises. Surmises that Lanier "achieved a
    kind of spaciousness of an illimitable horizon felt in the
    heart." Revised in 1946.B9.

9   _____. "Lanier, Inheritor of Unfulfilled Renown." New York
    Herald Tribune Weekly Book Review, XXIII (25 August), 1–2.
        Review of The Centennial Edition of the Works of Sidney
    Lanier. Discovers "the granitic restraint of an Emily
    Dickinson" and "Lindsay-like rhythms" in poems infrequently
    anthologized.

10 WILLIAMS, STANLEY T. "The Complete Lanier." Yale Review,
    XXXVI (Autumn), 179–181.
        Reviews The Centennial Edition of the Works of Sidney
    Lanier, discovering that Lanier is "now...required reading
    for us all." This edition is "at once the culmination of
    the increased study of Lanier and commencement of our real

evaluation of him," since he is the first writer "now in
the full dress of modern scholarship." Admires the editors'
"serenely judicious criticism" and wealth of notes.

11   WILSON, EDMUND. "Sidney Lanier and Stephen Foster."
      New Yorker, XXII (14 December), 134, 136, 138.
          Despite his provincial equipment and uninteresting mind,
      Lanier rose above his times with the assistance of Whitman,
      becoming, as Barrett Wendell said, "among the truest men of
      letters whom our country has produced." Reviews The Cen-
      tennial Edition of The Works of Sidney Lanier.

1947 A BOOKS - NONE

1947 B SHORTER WRITINGS

1   ANDERSON, CHARLES R. "Two Letters from Lanier to Holmes."
      American Literature, XVIII (January), 321–326.
          These cordial letters record views on satire and exten-
      sively summarize the relation of music and poetry, while
      hoping to append remarks on Holmes' prosodic theories in
      another edition of The Science of English Verse. The
      letters are from 1880.

2   _____. "Poet of the Pine Barrens." Georgia Review, I
      (Fall), 280–293.
          The central theme of forty-five letters between Hayne
      and Lanier (1868–1880) is the necessity of Southern poets
      to use the South as their subject. Hayne continually sup-
      ported Lanier, despite Lanier's frank review.

3   ANON. Review of Young's Selected Poems of Sidney Lanier.
      Kirkus, XV (15 August), 461.
          The "Introduction" is "fair and enthusiastic" and effec-
      tively shows the importance of music to his work. See
      1947.B13.

4   BRANTLEY, FREDERICK. "The Best of Lanier." New York Times,
      XCVII (7 December), Section 7, 6, 60.
          Decides that Lanier consciously styled his work on the
      image of the "sensitive artist" and wrote so much "senti-
      mental blather" about the artist that he failed to be one,
      and his work became inchoate. This "excessively self-con-
      scious preoccupation with the social role of the Poet" al-
      lowed Lanier to slip into "his cliches" of Science and the
      evils of Commerce. His pose of Artist and his clichés have
      accounted for his popularity and assure its continuance.
      See 1947.B13.

1947

5   BROOKS, VAN WYCK. <u>The Times of Melville and Whitman</u>.
     New York: Dutton, passim.
         Although Lanier settled in Baltimore, the mecca of
     Southerners, Georgia always remained "the subject of his
     most devoted thought." Loyal to the Georgia farmer and sen-
     sitive to the excesses of business, Lanier had a "passionate
     belief in his mission in the world"--a devotional sense more
     important than his poetry.

6   COULTER, E. MERTON. <u>The South During Reconstruction</u>.
     Baton Rouge: Louisiana State University Press, pp. 279-390.
         Provides valuable background material on Lanier's his-
     torical situation. "In the field of poetry appear the
     Southerners who came nearest to greatness."

7   GIBSON, C. D. "The Wonderful Marshes of Glynn." <u>Emory</u>
     <u>University Quarterly</u>, III (June), 116-121.
         Offers a scientific view of the geology and topology of
     the area inspiring Lanier's marsh poems.

8   LEARY, LEWIS. "The Forlorn Hope of Sidney Lanier." <u>South</u>
     <u>Atlantic Quarterly</u>, XLVI (April), 263-271.
         In this review of <u>The Centennial Edition of the Works of</u>
     <u>Sidney Lanier</u>, Leary finds the edition "complete" and the
     editors "unobtrusive and skillful." However, Lanier, as a
     "feeler" rather than a thinker, "seems never to have learned
     enough of language or himself to translate what he found of
     vision...into other than conventional generalities." Never-
     theless, "None need be ashamed of Sidney Lanier...unequivo-
     cally within the main current of American poetry."

9   MARVIN, PERRY, JR. "Keats in Georgia." <u>Georgia Review</u>, I
     (Winter), 460-470.
         Examines the similarity to Keats in Lanier's "Clover,"
     in which Keats is mentioned.

10   PAINE, GREGORY. <u>Southern Prose Writers</u>. New York: American
     Book, pp. 293-295, 390-391.
         Supplies a biographical note, while tracing the "liberal-
     izing" of Lanier's "Puritan ideas."

11   THORP, WILLARD. "A Memorial to Lanier." <u>Virginia Quarterly</u>
     <u>Review</u>, XXIII (Winter), 123-138.
         Reviews <u>The Centennial Edition of the Works of Sidney</u>
     <u>Lanier</u>, asserting that he "is an extraordinarily significant
     figure in the history of American culture" for what he re-
     veals of the American mind. From his eclectic novel to his
     <u>Florida</u> guidebook and his philological Johns Hopkins essays,

Lanier is remarkable for "turning weaknesses into
strengths," and inventing his own mythology.

12   WRIGHT, NATHALIA.   "The East Tennessee Background of Sidney
     Lanier's <u>Tiger Lilies</u>." <u>American Literature</u>, XIX (May),
     127–138.
          Shows that Lanier was quite accurate in his handling of
     Tennessee dialect and geography.

13   YOUNG, STARK, "Preface," in <u>Selected Poems of Sidney Lanier</u>.
     Edited by the author. New York: Charles Scribner's,
     pp. v–xiii.
          Lanier's admirers necessitated this edition. Surveys
     his life, finding that his poetry and music "mutually ab-
     sorbed" each other.

<u>1948 A BOOKS – NONE</u>

<u>1948 B SHORTER WRITINGS</u>

1   BROWN, CALVIN S. <u>Music and Literature</u>. Athens: University
     of Georgia Press, pp. 46–47, 171–172.
          Suggests that Lanier's notes to "The Centennial Cantata"
     imply that the poet should merely write notes for the com-
     poser's program music. Finds that "The Symphony" is too
     vague in form for one to detect if it is modeled on "a
     single movement or an entire symphony." Guesses that he
     had to make more "poetic sacrifices" than he wished in order
     to establish a real musical analogy.

2   C., M. S. Review of Young's <u>Selected Poems of Sidney Lanier</u>.
     <u>Kirkus</u>, XV (15 August), 461.
          Finds the "Introduction" fair but the poetry specialized.

3   EBY, E. HAROLD. Review of <u>The Centennial Edition of the Works
     of Sidney Lanier</u>. <u>Modern Language Quarterly</u>, IX (June),
     253.
          Proclaims the edition a model for other scholars to fol-
     low. Finds it tragic that Lanier did not have time to fully
     assimilate Emerson and Whitman.

4   GUEST, BOYD. "Sidney Lanier's Feminine Ideal." <u>Georgia
     Historical Quarterly</u>, XXXII (September), 175–178.
          Discovers that to Lanier woman was not a cold chivalric
     beauty but capable of great intelligence and love. While
     "The Symphony" promotes a single standard, Lanier thinks
     men better fit to grapple with the sordid realities.

1948

5   LANIER, MRS. W. D. "Sidney Lanier Committee." <u>United</u>
        <u>Daughters of the Confederacy Magazine</u>, XI (February), 8-9.
            Announcement that Mrs. Walter D. Lamar has been named
        chairman of the committee.

6   SCHOLL, EVELYN. "English Metre Once More." <u>Publications of</u>
        <u>the Modern Language Association</u>, LXIII (June), 293-326.
            Describes Lanier's prosodic interests within a general
        study of meter.

7   SHAPIRO, KARL. <u>A Bibliography of Modern Prosody</u>. Baltimore,
        Maryland: Johns Hopkins University Press, p. 16.
            <u>The Science of English Verse</u> is "justly the most famous
        and influential in the field of temporal prosody."

8   SPILLER, ROBERT E. "Sidney Lanier: Ancestor of Anti-Realism."
        <u>Saturday Review of Literature</u>, XXXI (10 January), 6-7, 24.
            Prompted by an essay on the decline of literary realism,
        sees Lanier as the precursor of neo-Romanticism.

9   WILLIAMS, STANLEY T. "Experiments in Poetry: Sidney Lanier
        and Emily Dickinson," in <u>Literary History of the United</u>
        <u>States</u>. Edited by Robert E. Spiller. New York: Macmillan,
        pp. 901-907.
            Finds Lanier's weaknesses to be mistiness, abstraction,
        sentimentality, and "far-fetched metaphors." His strengths
        reside in a "matchless pattern of sounds." Beyond this, he
        tried to suggest remedies for the excesses of industry, and
        thus pointed away from nostalgia for the Old South. His
        poetry represents a "feverish epitome" of the stirrings to-
        ward a new poetry in his "inconclusive gospel of the iden-
        tity of poetry and music."

10   WOOLEN, MRS. L. L. "Sidney Lanier." <u>United Daughters of the</u>
        <u>Confederacy Magazine</u>, XI (February), 10-11.
            Records the dedication of Lanier's bust in the Hall of
        Fame.

1949 A BOOKS - NONE

1949 B SHORTER WRITINGS

1   CONNER, FREDERICK W. <u>Cosmic Optimism</u>. Gainesville:
        University of Florida Press, pp. 199-210.
            Relying on his early work, traces Lanier's concern for
        synthesis in the arts and etherealization of his age. He
        calls Lanier in this regard a "son of his Age."

2   DANIEL, ROBERT N. "Sidney Lanier." Furman Studies, XXXI
      (Winter), 35-45.
         Biographical sketch, stressing socially constructive
      ideas.

3   FLETCHER, JOHN GOULD. "Sidney Lanier." University of Kansas
      City Review, XVI (Winter), 97-102.
         Both he and Conrad Aiken wished to adapt "symphonic de-
      velopment and construction" to poetic form.

4   OSTERWEIS, ROLLIN G. Romanticism and Nationalism in the Old
      South. New Haven, Connecticut: Yale University Press,
      pp. 52, 105.
         Represented "the culmination of the chivalric theme in
      Southern romantic literature."

1950 A BOOKS - NONE

1950 B SHORTER WRITINGS

1   BROOKS, CLEANTH and ROBERT PENN WARREN. Understanding Poetry.
      New York: Henry Holt, pp. 297-302.
         Dub Lanier's "My Springs" strained and sentimental, with
      arbitrary relations of images which are not functional.

1951 A BOOKS - NONE

1951 B SHORTER WRITINGS

1   ANDERSON, CHARLES R. "Lanier and Science: Addenda." Modern
      Language Notes, LXVI (June), 395-398.
         Describes four poem outlines: one criticizes Sir William
      Hamilton's view of knowledge; another equates love with God.

2   GOHDES, CLARENCE. "Sidney Lanier," in The Literature of the
      American People. Edited by Arthur H. Quinn. New York:
      Appleton-Century-Crofts, pp. 632-636.
         Places Lanier's prose in its science, music, and German
      literature contexts.

3   TANKERSLEY, ALLEN P. College Life at Old Oglethorpe. Athens:
      University of Georgia Press, passim.
         Informative description of the college with a list of
      books Lanier used in courses he attended.

1951

4   TODD, EDGELEY. "The Literary Relationship of Sidney Lanier
      and his Father." <u>Western Humanities Review</u>, V (Spring),
      175–194.
          The father guided the son's taste in his formative years.

<u>1952 A BOOKS – NONE</u>

<u>1952 B SHORTER WRITINGS</u>

1   BEATTY, RICHARD C.; FLOYD WATKINS; THOMAS D. YOUNG; and
      RANDALL STEWART. <u>The Literature of the South</u>. New York:
      Scott, Foresman, pp. 441–443, 515–516.
          Though Lanier was the important poet of the Reconstruc-
      tion South, his criticism represented a "considerable
      achievement," particularly <u>The Science of English Verse</u>.

2   BROOKS, VAN WYCK. <u>The Confident Years: 1885–1915</u>. New York:
      E. P. Dutton Inc., p. 426.
          Places Lanier in the American grain with his hope that
      Macon would become an art center of the future.

<u>1953 A BOOKS</u>

1   WHITTEMORE, MYRTLE. <u>Flute Concerto of Sidney Lanier</u>.
      New York: Pagent Press, 301pp.
          Fictionalizes Lanier's life, basing her imagined conver-
      sations and dramatized scenes on his letters.

<u>1953 B SHORTER WRITINGS</u>

1   BEAVER, JOSEPH. "Lanier's Use of Science for Poetic Imagery."
      <u>American Literature</u>, XXIV (January), 520–523.
          Explains various scientific ideas, their origin and ex-
      tensiveness, in Lanier's work.

2   CANBY, HENRY; ROBERT SPILLER; WILLIAM THORPE; and THOMAS
      JOHNSON. <u>Literary History of the United States:</u>
      <u>Bibliographical Supplements</u>. New York: Macmillan,
      pp. 605–608.
          Lists significant items related to Lanier, primary and
      secondary.

3   FALK, ROBERT P. "The Rise of Realism, 1871–1891," in
      <u>Transitions in American Literary History</u>. Edited by Harry
      Hayden Clark. Durham, North Carolina: Duke University
      Press, pp. 411–415.

Asserts that Lanier created a synthesis of Darwinian and aesthetic concerns. His critical work sought to treat all issues raised by Realism--the relation of the arts, the quest for a science of criticism, and the relation of science to literature. Thus, Lanier resembled Henry James.

4   WILLIAMS, WILLIAM CARLOS. "The Present Relationship of Prose to Verse." Seven Arts, I:140–149.
    Finds The Science of English Verse to be "Extremely interesting and well worth study," mainly because Lanier recognized "it is the question of time in the make-up of the modern line that has to be wrestled with." Particularly interested in suggestions of Lanier's related to the development of English rhythms away from the iambic line.

1954 A BOOKS - NONE

1954 B SHORTER WRITINGS

1   BETTS, WILLIAM. "The Fortunes of Faust in American Literature." Ph.D. Dissertation, Pennsylvania State University.
    Traces connections between Tiger-Lilies and Goethe's Faust.

2   CALLAHAN, NORTH. "The Life of Sidney Lanier as Related to His Work." Southern Observer, II (August), 169–178.
    Biographically-oriented survey of Lanier's work.

3   HARDING, WALTER. "Sidney Lanier and Virginia Hankins: Two Letters." Georgia Historical Quarterly, XXXVIII (September), 290–294.
    These two letters from Mary Day to Virginia Hankins and from Hankins to Lanier show how the inter-relations of these people created a "complex problem." Mary Day called Lanier their "mutual pledge," uniting the trio in friendship.

4   HUBBELL, JAY B. The South in American Literature: 1607–1900. Durham, North Carolina: Duke University Press, pp. 758–777.
    Notes in an historical survey of Lanier's development that the later poetry lacks the simplicity of his early work, perhaps because he was fundamentally an improvisor, not a craftsman.

5   SVENDSEN, KESTER. "Lanier's Cone of Night: An Early Poetic Commonplace." American Literature, XXVI (March), 93–94.
    Corrects an error in Beaver's view of Lanier's use of scientific imagery. See 1953.B1.

1955

1955 A BOOKS - NONE

1955 B SHORTER WRITINGS

    1   CANTRELL, CLYDE and WALTON PATRICK. <u>Southern Literary Culture</u>.
        Birmingham: University of Alabama Press, p. 112.
           The editors list 107 theses and dissertations concerning
        Lanier. Each is identified in this index according to its
        subject, and other writers treated in the theses and disser-
        tations are identified.

    2   SCHOLES, PERCY A. <u>The Oxford Companion to Music</u>. Ninth
        edition. New York: Oxford University Press, p. 570.
           The musicality of Lanier's ancestors was "still aflame"
        in the "decidedly musical flow" of his poetry.

    3   SPILLER, ROBERT E. <u>The Cycle of American Literature</u>.
        New York: Macmillan, pp. 158-159.
           Asserts that Lanier clearly reveals "the effort at the
        turn of the century to make poetry in the image of science,"
        in critical theory as well as in poetic practice. Modern
        poets owe him more than they admit, since he helped provide
        a fresh study of the laws of verse.

    4   STOVALL, FLOYD. <u>The Development of American Literary
        Criticism</u>. Chapel Hill: University of North Carolina
        Press, passim.
           <u>The English Novel</u> shows "the twilight of transcendental
        thought in criticism."

1956 A BOOKS - NONE

1956 B SHORTER WRITINGS

    1   BROOKS, VAN WYCK and OTTO L. BETTMANN. "Sidney Lanier," in
        <u>Our Literary Heritage</u>. New York: E. P. Dutton, pp. 134-136.
           Although a "curious unreality" in Southern writers, typi-
        fied by Lanier's chivalry, kept them from national promi-
        nence, Lanier became "the first real voice emerging from
        the New South."

    2   GREEN, DAVID. "Two Letters of Sidney Lanier." <u>Maryland
        Historical Magazine</u>, LI (March), 54-56.
           Lanier writes to Gibson Peacock in gratitude for his en-
        thusiasm over "Corn," and in the other letter he explores
        the possibility of publishing "How to Read Chaucer."

3   HOWELL, RONALD F. "Poet Bleckley, Friend of Sidney Lanier."
    Georgia Review, X (Fall), 321–332.
        Recounts how Judge Bleckley encouraged Lanier to revise
    "Corn" in 1874.

4   LENHART, CHARMENZ. Musical Influence on American Poetry.
    Athens: University of Georgia Press, pp. 210–292, 309–313.
        Notes aspects of music throughout Lanier's work, calling
    him "the only professional musician in the annals of Ameri-
    can poetry to achieve real fame as a poet." Discusses how
    Lanier used "leitmotifs" in Tiger-Lilies, and how he at-
    tempted to model "The Symphony" on the musical form of a
    symphony. Contends that because of his musical experiences
    of the 1870's, his best poetry was written after 1874, and
    further asserts that The Science of English Verse has been
    largely substantiated. Analyzes many of Lanier's poems to
    show how carefully he contrived the musicality of his verse,
    concluding that "The Symphony" is an uneven experiment and
    "The Centennial Cantata" revealed sensitivity in the han-
    dling of music and poetry in combination. His very last
    poems show a virtuoso handling of the musical resources of
    poetry.

5   LEWIS, ARTHUR O., JR. "Sidney Lanier's Study of German."
    American-German Review, XXII (March), 30–32.
        Examines Tiger-Lilies for clues to Lanier's use of
    German Romance.

6   TAYLOR, WALTER F. The Story of American Letters. Chicago:
    Henry Regnery, pp. 252–255.
        Reprint of 1936.B15.

1957 A BOOKS – NONE

1957 B SHORTER WRITINGS

1   HOGENES, ELIZABETH. "Lanier's 'The Symphony, 326–368.'"
    Explicator, XVI (October), item 4.
        Detects regression in time and progress from city to sea
    in "The Symphony."

2   LEWIS, ARTHUR O., JR. "Sidney Lanier's Knowledge of German
    Literature." Anglo-German and American-German Cross-
    currents, I:155–158.
        Considers the impact of German Romanticism to have been
    extensive. Offers sources of Lanier's borrowings.

1957

3   POCHMAN, HENRY A. German Culture in America. Madison:
         University of Wisconsin Press, pp. 460–461, 776–777.
            Traces German themes in Tiger-Lilies. The famous thought
         that "music is love" is of German origin. Describes his
         German friends and speculates on the importance of Carlyle's
         German essays.

1958 A BOOKS - NONE

1958 B SHORTER WRITINGS

1   BROOKE, BISSELL. "Memorial Day Tribute to a Famous Author."
         Hobbies, LXIII (May), 108–109, 121.
            Describes Lanier's relation to Robert E. Lee.

2   PARKS, EDD W. "Lanier's 'Night and Day.'" American
         Literature, XXX (March), 117–118.
            Sees the poem as a Civil War allegory.

3   STEWART, RANDALL. American Literature and Christian Doctrine.
         Baton Rouge: Louisiana State University Press, pp. 65–69.
            Lanier used conventional religious imagery, and, despite
         his interest in "progressivism, scientism, liberalism, na-
         turalism, and the like," it is doubtful that he ever aban-
         doned "the basic Christian tenets." Contends that "A Ballad
         of Trees and the Master" and "The Marshes of Glynn" show
         that in an Age of "pantheistic nature poetry, Lanier's God
         is not submerged in the natural world."

4   THOMPSON, OSCAR. "Sidney Lanier," in The International
         Cyclopedia of Music and Musicians. Eighth revised edition.
         New York: Dodd, Mead, pp. 977–978.
            Surveys Lanier's flute-playing and his music-related
         poetry, but not his musical compositions.

1959 A BOOKS - NONE

1959 B SHORTER WRITINGS

1   BLANCO, MANUEL GARCÍA. "Unamuno y tres poetas norteamericanos."
         Asomante, XV (April–June), 39–44.
            Unamuno's Cancionero shows the influence of Lanier's
         marsh poems.

2   GRAHAM, PHILIP. "Sidney Lanier and the Pattern of Contrast."
         American Quarterly, XI (Winter), 503–508.

Uses statistics to show that Lanier used patterns of contrast in his work more often than any other Southern writer.

3   HENDREN, JOSEPH W.   "Time and Stress in English Verse with
Special Reference to Lanier's Theory of Rhythm."   Rice
Institute Pamphlets, XLVI (July), 1-72.
Seeks to rescue Lanier's significant work from discredit,
and so lists conventional errors of prosodic analysis in
supporting the contentions of The Science of English Verse.
Indicates that his great fault was in attempting to con-
struct a musical theory within the traditional use of the
"barred foot"--something his own theory totally denied.

4   LUDWIG, RICHARD M.   "Bibliography Supplement," in Literary
History of the United States.   Edited by Robert E. Spiller,
et al.   New York: Macmillan, pp. 153-154.
Listing of items for the years 1947-1956.

5   SHIPHERD, THOMAS.   Collection of Indexes to Selected Works.
Southold, New York: privately published, 15pp.
An index to Lanier's letters.

6   WHITE, WILLIAM.   "Sidney Lanier as a Critic."   Today's Japan,
IV (March), 41-44.
General survey of Lanier's attempted integrations of re-
ligion and science, music and poetry.   Confines itself en-
tirely to the criticism, with a summary of The Science of
English Verse.

7   WILLIAMS, WILLIAM CARLOS.   "Measure."   Spectrum, III (Fall),
131-157.
Identifies The Science of English Verse as "a wholly in-
adequate and untenable division of the measure into musical
pauses."

1960 A BOOKS - NONE

1960 B SHORTER WRITINGS

1   HOWARD, LEON.   Literature and the American Tradition.
New York: Doubleday, pp. 190-191.
Argues that Lanier needed to "escape" emotionally into
"the conventional channels of an earlier period"--the past,
nature, and the glorification of emotion over reason.   "The
Symphony" summarizes the resources open to the South in
withstanding materialism.

1960

2   JONES, DAVID. "Clifford Anderson Lanier." Georgia Review,
    XIV (Summer), 205–214.
        Describes how Clifford lent his brother continual finan-
    cial support. Finds his best work to be the eight sonnets
    to Sidney Lanier, 1875.

3   JONES, JOSEPH. "Sidney Lanier," in American Literary
    Manuscripts. Austin: University of Texas Press,
    pp. 213–214.
        Lists the libraries where Lanier manuscripts may be
    found.

4   KEATING, L. CLARK. "Francis Viele-Griffin and America."
    Symposium, XIV (Winter), 276–281.
        This transplanted American "Symbolist" poet translated
    Lanier's "Life and Song" into French.

5   MAYFIELD, JOHN S. "Lanier in the Florae: or, What Would You
    Have Done?" American Book Collector, X (February), 7–10.
        Recounts how he purchased ten mis-shelved copies of
    Tiger-Lilies in the botany section of a bookstore.

6   ROVIT, EARL. "James Joyce's Use of Sidney Lanier." Notes and
    Queries, CCV (April), 151.
        Joyce included the Chattahoochee river in Finnegans Wake.

1961 A BOOKS - NONE

1961 B SHORTER WRITINGS

1   PEARCE, ROY HARVEY. The Continuity of American Poetry.
    Princeton, New Jersey: Princeton University Press,
    pp. 236–246.
        Discovers Lanier's later poetry "confused regarding its
    aims, its putative audience, and its form and its media."
    His experiments only removed him from the tradition which
    sustained later, better poets like Ransom, Tate and Warren.
    Lanier's crisis was the same as that of all nineteenth-
    century American poets, only intensified by the collapse of
    the South. Tied to the traditions of "public poetry" Lanier
    could not move toward "pure poetry" as Poe did, nor could
    he become a poet "of the antimonian self" like Whitman.

2   ROSS, ROBERT H. "'The Marshes of Glynn': A Study in Symbolic
    Obscurity." American Literature, XXXII (January), 403–416.
        Suggests that Lanier creates an imbalance between his
    key symbols of woods, marsh, and sea. He finds the poem

confused when Lanier writes, at the end, of the tide as "waters of sleep." The falling of night, he argues, would better end the poem, completing its "existential experience" and revealing that Lanier, like other nineteenth century writers, doubted the efficacy of "seeing God in everything."

1962 A BOOKS - NONE

1962 B SHORTER WRITINGS

1   FLORY, CLAUDE R. "Paul Hamilton Hayne and the New South."
    Georgia Historical Quarterly, XLVI (December), 388-394.
        Notes that Hayne did not agree with Lanier's feeling of
    national hope in "The Psalm of the West."

2   KEEFER, LUBOV. Baltimore's Music. Baltimore, Maryland:
    J. H. Furst, pp. 178-188.
        Notes that at Oglethorpe flute and banjo were his "alter
    ego." His favorite poetic form was "attraction and repul-
    sion," a musical form. Keefer places him in the context of
    the Baltimore musical world of the 1870's.

3   PARKS, EDD W. Ante-Bellum Southern Literary Critics. Athens:
    University of Georgia Press, pp. 108-109, 338-339.
        Parks notes William Gilmore Simms' favorable review of
    Tiger-Lilies.

4   WILSON, EDMUND. Patriotic Gore. New York: Oxford University
    Press, pp. 450-466, 519-528.
        With long extracts from his letters and Tiger-Lilies,
    Wilson illustrates how Lanier gave the "most poetic" vision
    of the Southern myth, comprised of "hallowed ideal of gal-
    lantry, aristocratic freedom, fine manners." Although he
    finds his "nobility" boring and his criticism "sometimes a
    little stupid," Wilson dubs him among the "truest" American
    men of letters. He also identifies Civil War "parables" in
    "The Jacquerie" and "The Revenge of Hamish."

1963 A BOOKS

1   FISH, TALLU. Sidney Lanier: America's Sweetest Singer of
    Songs. Darien, Georgia: Darien News, 22pp.
        The author, whose mother helped install Lanier in the
    Hall of Fame, supplies an appreciative "Foreword," a brief
    biography and chronology, notes to several poems, and many
    illustrations. She seeks to show how Lanier "touched our
    lives in many ways."

1963

1963 B SHORTER WRITINGS

1 ABEL, DARREL. American Literature. Vol. II. Woodbury,
New York: Barron's Educational Series, pp. 498-517.
Argues that a blend of Puritanism and "sham-chivalry" of
the Old South united in Lanier to produce the first Southern
poet of national importance. As a Cavalier poet, he adhered
to sectional and national duty. As a Puritan, he examined
nature and cross-examined himself for indications of spiritual continuity. Abel examines his major work in pursuing
this view, concluding that Lanier's "prudishness and silli-
ness about chivalry" kept him from the "gristly stuff" that
characterized Whitman and could have strengthened him. Yet
Lanier was "one of the best half-dozen American poets of
the 19th century," and, given his adversities, "achieved
more heroically than any other."

1964 A BOOKS

1 DE BELLIS, JACK ANGELO. Sidney Lanier and the Morality of
Feeling. Ph.D. Dissertation, University of California at
Los Angeles, 360pp.
Argues that Lanier's life work can be understood as a
series of projects undertaken to define the morality of
feeling. In his novel he allegorized his hero and villain
as "heart" and "brain," as he had done in chivalric poetry
written shortly after the Civil War. In "The Symphony" he
placed in various musical instruments didactic passages
condemning the errors of "brain" (materialism, economic exploitation, indifference to nature) and defending values of
"heart" through quotations from St. Paul as well as sharp
depictions of nature. Afterwards, while a performing musician in Baltimore, Lanier sought to intensify the musicality
of his verse. By making poetry resemble music, he reasoned,
he would be able to affect the "heart" of his audience and
thus turn his Age away from "brain." In "The Marshes of
Glynn" this strategy produced a state of feeling which,
coupled to the ancient theme of the quest into nature,
projected the feeling of a transcendental state.

2 STARKE, AUBREY. Sidney Lanier: A Biographical and Critical
Study. New York: Russell and Russell, 525pp.
Reprint of 1933.A1.

1964 B SHORTER WRITINGS

1 ABERNETHY, CECIL. "Lanier in Alabama." <u>Alabama Review</u>, XVII
   (January), 5–21.
       Recounts Lanier's Alabama contacts--working at his
   uncle's Montgomery hotel, playing a flute concert for the
   Montgomery Literary Society, and teaching at Prattville
   Academy, a job which left him weak and destitute.

2 DE BELLIS, JACK ANGELO. "Sidney Lanier and the Morality of
   Feeling." <u>Dissertation Abstracts</u>, XXV, 1907.
       <u>See</u> 1964.A1.

3 ENGLAND, KENNETH. "Sidney Lanier in C Major," in <u>Reality and
   Myth: Essays in American Literature in Memory of Richard
   Croom Beatty</u>. Edited by William E. Walker and Robert L.
   Welker. Nashville, Tennessee: Vanderbilt University
   Press, pp. 60–70.
       Asserts that Lanier's "progressive" thoughts concerning
   nationalism and the "New South" were reversed in his poetry.
   He was "basically of the conviction of the old Southerner."

4 MERIDETH, ROBERT. "Emily Dickinson and the Acquisitive
   Society." <u>New England Quarterly</u>, XXXVII (December),
   435–452.
       Notes that the percentage of Dickinson's poems "chime"
   with the theme of the poor's exploitation in Lanier's "The
   Symphony."

5 PARKS, EDD W. <u>Henry Timrod</u>. United States Authors Series,
   no. 53. New York: Twayne, pp. 109–110, 144.
       Parks evaluates Lanier's criticism of Timrod as essen-
   tially unsound, perhaps even unfair, since he asserted that
   Timrod was not a craftsman.

1965 A BOOKS

1 HAVENS, ELMER. "Sidney Lanier's Concept and Use of Nature."
   Ph.D. Dissertation, University of Wisconsin.
       Examines Lanier's use of the theory of etherealization
   and finds that it exhibited not only his chief poetic concern, but also played a major part in his social and aesthetic interests. Abstracted in 1965.B6.

1965

1965 B SHORTER WRITINGS

1   ANON. "The Poet of the South," in <u>The Lanier Library, 1890–</u>
    <u>1965</u>. Tryon, North Carolina: printed privately,
    pp. vii–xiv.
        Supplies a popular biography of the poet for whom this
    library was named in 1955.

2   ATCHISON, RAY M. "<u>Scott's Monthly Magazine</u>: A Georgia
    Post-Bellum Periodical of Literature and Military History."
    <u>Georgia Historical Quarterly</u>, XLIX (September), 294–305.
        Shows how the magazine helped to launch Lanier's career
    by publishing "Raven Days" and the essay "The Three Water-
    falls."

3   BROWN, CALVIN S. "Can Musical Notation Help English Scansion?"
    <u>Journal of Aesthetics and Art Criticism</u>, XXIII (Spring),
    329–334.
        Decides that the system of musical notation used in <u>The</u>
    <u>Science of English Verse</u> has very limited applications.

4   HALL, WADE. <u>The Smiling Phoenix: Southern Humor from 1865–</u>
    <u>1914</u>. Gainesville: University of Florida Press, pp. 32–33,
    98–99, 192–193, 243–244.
        Examines the humor of the dialect poems.

5   HART, JAMES D. "Sidney Lanier." <u>Oxford Companion to American</u>
    <u>Literature</u>. New York: Oxford University Press, pp. 455–456.
        Biographical sketch stressing Lanier's musical progeni-
    tors.

6   HAVENS, ELMER A. "Sidney Lanier's Concept and Use of Nature."
    <u>Dissertation Abstracts</u>, XXV, 7268.
        <u>See</u> 1965.A1.

7   PREMINGER, ALEX. <u>Encyclopedia of Poetry and Poetics</u>.
    Princeton, New Jersey: Princeton University Press, p. 26.
        Biographical sketch.

8   WARFEL, HARRY R. "Mystic Vision in 'The Marshes of Glynn.'"
    <u>Mississippi Quarterly</u>, XIX (Winter), 39–40.
        Analyzes the poem, showing that in its structure it pre-
    sents a coherent vision of the fusion of the soul with God.
    A chart shows the syntax, tense, time-scheme and narrative
    action of the poem. <u>See</u> 1969.B8.

1966 A BOOKS - NONE

1966 B SHORTER WRITINGS

1   WILLIAMS, JOHN J.   "Hamlin Garland's 'Sidney Lanier.'"
    English Language Notes, III (June), 282–283.
        A twenty-nine line elegy on Lanier by Garland reprinted
    from Southern Bivouac, May, 1887.

1967 A BOOKS - NONE

1967 B SHORTER WRITINGS

1   HARRISON, STANLEY R.   "Through a Nineteenth-Century Looking
    Glass: The Letters of Edgar Fawcett." Tulane Studies in
    English, XV:107-157.
        Though he changed his mind, Fawcett at first was shocked
    and disgusted by Lanier's "artistic insolence."

2   HOWARD, CHESTER JERIEL.   "Sidney Lanier in 1967."
    Dissertation Abstracts, XXIX, 2712A.
        Sees Lanier in the roles of Southerner, agrarian, reli-
    gious poet, and authority on versification. Insists that
    balanced criticism must see him as both an innovative proso-
    dist and as a Southern poet writing about Southern ideas and
    people in Southern settings. Offers three chapters treating
    Lanier's life and the South, two chapters on his use of
    "Southern matter," three chapters on his social, religious
    and literary themes, and three chapters charting trends in
    scholarship.

3   MARTIN, JAY.   "Sidney Lanier: The Real and the Ideal," in
    Harvests of Change: American Literature 1865-1914.
    Englewood Cliffs, New Jersey: Prentice Hall, pp. 92-96.
        Committed to the myth of the Old South, Lanier idealized
    chivalry as a New Eden. Expelling the serpent of Trade from
    the Garden, he anticipated Kropotkin by stressing coopera-
    tion not conflict in nature, and he foreshadowed Veblen by
    emphasizing good will rather than power.

4   OWEN, GUY.   "Southern Poetry During the 30's," in The Thirties:
    Fiction, Poetry, Drama. Edited by Warren French. Deland,
    Florida: Everett Edwards, pp. 159-167.
        The Fugitive poets forced a revaluation of Lanier.

5   PARKS, EDD W.   "Lanier as Poet," in Essays on American
    Literature in Honor of Jay B. Hubbell. Edited by Clarence

1968

Gohdes. Durham, North Carolina: Duke University Press, pp. 183–201.
Since he never outgrew his tendencies to didacticism and artificiality, and because personal and circumstantial obstacles intruded, he never became "even a major American poet." Reprinted in 1968.A2.

1968 A BOOKS

1 MIMS, EDWIN. Sidney Lanier. Port Washington, New York: Kennicat Press, 386pp.
Reprint of 1905.A1.

2 PARKS, EDD WINFIELD. Sidney Lanier: The Man, The Poet, The Critic. Athens: University of Georgia Press, 103pp.
"The Man" provides a biographical up-date, adhering closely to authenticated facts. "The Poet" reviews the obstacles which prevented Lanier from achieving greatness, although the "philosophical content" and "musical form" of his later poems overrode his weaknesses. "The Critic" emphasizes that Lanier "was neither a logical nor a consistent critic," by revealing his moralistic view of fiction and his allegorizing of Shakespeare's plays. Charts his attitudes toward noted writers and offers an extensive survey of The Science of English Verse. "The Poet" is a reprint of 1967.B5.

1968 B SHORTER WRITINGS

1 DABNEY, JULIA P. The Musical Basis of Verse. New York: Greenwood, passim.
Reprint of 1901.B1.

2 DE BELLIS, JACK ANGELO. "Sidney Lanier and German Romance: An Important Qualification." Comparative Literature Studies, V (June), 145–155.
Corrects a mistaken over-estimation of German Romance's influence on Tiger-Lilies. Rejects the view that the book was strongly influenced by Novalis by showing that Lanier's entire knowledge of German Romance resided in his reading of Carlyle's essays. Suggests that those essays provided inspiration for Faustian elements in Tiger-Lilies.

3 EATON, CLEMENT. The Waning of the Old South Civilization, 1860–1880's. Athens: University of Georgia Press, pp. 79–81, 99–101, 123–125.

1969

Attributes to Lanier the thought that a glorious era of culture would result from Southern Confederacy.

4   EDWARDS, JOHN S. "Sidney Lanier: Musical Pioneer." Georgia Review, XXII (Winter), 473–481.
        Although his musical compositions were unoriginal, he helped improve the position of American music by his position as a flute virtuoso.

5   KRAMER, AARON. The Prophetic Tradition in American Poetry, 1835–1900. Rutherford, New Jersey: Fairleigh Dickinson University Press, pp. 252–253.
        Construes Lanier's praise of progress to be self-serving.

6   OMOND, THOMAS STEWART. English Metrists. New York: Phaeton Press, pp. 195–202.
        Reprint of 1921.B3.

7   SIMMS, L. MOODY, JR. "A Note on Sidney Lanier's Attitude Toward the Negro and Toward Populism." Georgia Historical Quarterly, LII (September), 305–307.
        Indicating the future of the New South, Lanier stressed the unity of white and black farmers—a fundamental alliance of the Populist Movement.

8   WAGGONER, HYATT H. American Poets: From the Puritans to the Present. Boston: Houghton Mifflin, pp. 225–240.
        This "least bad" Southern poet held complacent views of God and Nature, as well as misconceptions about the musicality of verse.

1969 A BOOKS - NONE

1969 B SHORTER WRITINGS

1   ANDERSON, CHARLES R. "Introduction," in Sidney Lanier: Poems and Letters. Baltimore, Maryland: Johns Hopkins University Press, pp. 1–15, 75–88.
        Although the texts and notes of the poems and letters are the same as those Anderson used in The Centennial Edition of the Works of Sidney Lanier, Anderson says his essay was written "especially for this volume." However, it is essentially the same as the original "Introduction," though it emphasizes Lanier's effort to attach himself to the concrete realities of life. A revision of 1945.B1.

1969

2   ANON. "The Length and the Breadth and the Sweep of the Marshes
      of Glynn." Life, LXVII (14 November), 88–93.
         Emphasizing the poetic use Lanier made of the area, draws
      attention to efforts to forestall its exploitation.

3   GRAHAM, PHILIP and JOSEPH JONES. A Concordance to the Poems
      of Sidney Lanier. New York: Johnson Reprint Corporation,
      447pp.
         Reprint of 1939.B2.

4   HARWELL, RICHARD. "Introduction," in Tiger-Lilies: A Novel.
      Chapel Hill: University of North Carolina Press,
      pp. vii–xiii.
         This introduction to the reprinting of the original edi-
      tion of the novel describes it as "intensely interesting"
      for revelations about the author. Provides an account of
      its inception, contrasts it to Clifford Lanier's Thorn-
      Fruit, compares it to other Civil War novels, and agrees
      with De Bellis (1968.B2) that the impact of German Romance
      on the novel had been misunderstood.

5   HAVENS, ELMER A. "Lanier's Critical Theory." Emerson Society
      Quarterly, LV, no. 2, 83–89.
         To Lanier the artist was "the moral superman." The
      greatest of these was Shakespeare. Links his moral view of
      art to etherealization and evolutionism.

6   LEASE, BENJAMIN. "Sidney Lanier and Blackwood's Magazine: An
      Unpublished Letter." Georgia Historical Quarterly, LIII
      (December), 521–523.
         Lanier sought to publish an essay showing how America
      was being converted from a store-house to a wasteland.

7   PARKS, EDD W. and HARRY WARFEL. "Sidney Lanier," in A
      Bibliographical Guide to the Study of Southern Literature.
      Edited by Louis D. Rubin, Jr. Baton Rouge: Louisiana State
      University Press, pp. 236–237.
         List about thirty items comprising the best Lanier
      scholarship through 1968.

8   REAMER, OWEN J. "Lanier's 'Marshes of Glynn' Revisited."
      Mississippi Quarterly, XXIII (May), 57–63.
         Rejects Warfel's reading (1965.B8) of the poem as mystic
      vision, instead contending that Lanier reaffirms God's
      existence through nature symbols.

9   RIBBENS, DENNIS NEIL. "The Reading Interests of Thoreau,
      Hawthorne, and Lanier." Dissertation Abstracts Inter-
      national, XXXI, 777A.

Describes Lanier's reading as containing "multiple radices" linked to the other writers. The unifying force of his reading was his "philosophy of synthesis."

10 RUBIN, LOUIS D., JR. "The Image of an Army: The Civil War in Southern Fiction," in Southern Writers: Appraisals in Our Time. Edited by R. C. Simonini, Jr. Freeport, New York: Books for Libraries Press, pp. 50–51.
Like similar shelfloads of Southern Civil War fiction, Tiger-Lilies was "wretched stuff."

11 WRIGHT, NATHALIA. "Edd Winfield Parks on Sidney Lanier." Southern Literary Journal, II (Fall), 152–157.
Supplies a description but not a criticism of 1968.A2.

1970 A BOOKS - NONE

1970 B SHORTER WRITINGS

1 BLANCK, JACOB. Bibliography of American Literature. Vol. V. New Haven, Connecticut: Yale University Press, pp. 298–328.
Describes all editions of Lanier's work as well as books which include his work.

2 EDELSTEIN, TILDEN G. Strange Enthusiasm: A Life of Thomas Wentworth Higginson. New York: Atheneum, pp. 355–357.
After his unfavorable review of Poems (1877), he extolled Lanier as the great Southern poet, a "master singer." Higginson championed the chivalric "Symphony" against the "fleshy" Leaves of Grass. Lanier was the "Sir Galahad of American poets."

3 FRIEDL, HERWIG. "Poe und Lanier: Ein Vergleich ihrer Verdichtung." Jahrbuch für Amerikastudien, XV:123–140.
Observes that unlike Poe, Lanier had no dominant pattern of rhythms in his later poems, and he holds objects together by "an empathic feeling that reaches religious intensity," rather than by Poe's fusion of objects in abnormal situations.

4 GREENBURG, FRANK J. "Cultural Neurosis in the South: Sidney Lanier: Romantic? or Revolutionary?" November Review (Brooklyn), VI (Spring), 7–22.
Charts Lanier's reactions to the "shock waves" of change.

1971

<u>1971 A BOOKS – NONE</u>

<u>1971 B SHORTER WRITINGS</u>

   1   GRAHAM, PHILIP. "Sidney Lanier." <u>Encyclopedia Britannica</u>.
        Vol. XI. Chicago: William Benton, p. 706.
           Surveys Lanier's life and finds he is most important as
       a "transitional" figure.

   2   HARBERT, EARL N. and ROBERT A. REES. <u>Fifteen American Authors</u>
        <u>Before 1900</u>. Madison: University of Wisconsin Press,
        p. 403.
           Contains "the more important" items of Lanier criticism.

   3   KIMBALL, WILLIAM J. "Realism in Sidney Lanier's <u>Tiger-Lilies</u>."
        <u>South Atlantic Bulletin</u>, XXXVI (March), 17–20.
           This is an impressive novel because of its verisimilitude
       in characterization and prison scenes.

<u>1972 A BOOKS</u>

   1   DE BELLIS, JACK ANGELO. <u>Sidney Lanier</u>. United States Authors
        Series, no. 205. New York: Twayne, 169pp.
           Examines Lanier's growth through an analysis of his grow-
       ing sensitivity to the ways in which poetry could be made
       to express the "morality of feeling." Working in obedience
       to his dream of educating the emotions, with "The Symphony"
       (1875) he discovered a way to symbolize the conflict between
       feeling and thought as a conflict between love and material-
       ism. By casting this poem in such a way that orchestral
       instruments would appear to utter various attitudes, he
       subtly injected great feeling for his sense of the dualism
       of his age through the musicality of his verse. His analy-
       sis of the musical basis of poetry in <u>The Science of English</u>
       <u>Verse</u> exposed his intention of placing the poet's intuitive
       sense of musicality on empirical foundations. In this way
       his ability to stimulate his audience would be greater,
       hence the inculcating of the morality of feeling would ad-
       vance. "The Marshes of Glynn" and "Sunrise" show how rhythm
       experiment was used to re-inforce the portrait of spiritual
       recovery as his narrators learned the deepest morality
       through Nature.

<u>1972 B SHORTER WRITINGS</u>

   1   EDWARDS, C. H. "Lanier's 'The Symphony,' 64-84." <u>Explicator</u>,
        XXXI (December), item 27.

Argues that the rhyming words of this passage are analogous to musical modulation.

2   ____. "The Sea in Four Romantic Poems." West Georgia
      College Review, V (May), 29–34.
         Finds congruence in the work of Poe, Whitman, Wordsworth,
      and "The Marshes of Glynn."

3   HOLMAN, C. HUGH. The Roots of Southern Writing. Athens:
      University of Georgia Press, pp. 7, 189.
         In widely separated contexts, Holman offers two insights:
      The Science of English Verse came from the Southern tradi-
      tion of interest in the intrinsic qualities and technical
      aspects of literature; and, Lanier's poetry tended to sup-
      port the new economic order after the Civil War.

4   HUBBELL, JAY B. Who Are the Major American Writers? Durham:
      University of North Carolina Press, pp. 116, 239, 242, 278.
         Indicates that Lanier's reputation has gradually risen
      among critics during the past century. W. D. Howells was
      clearly mistaken in rejecting "Corn," and other critics were
      slow to see that like Whitman and Dickinson, Lanier also ran
      counter to the timid poetic conventions of his time. Mat-
      thiessen's view in 1950 that Timrod was superior to Lanier
      has not been upheld, and George Arms in 1953 considered the
      New England poets no better than Lanier. After being down-
      graded in the second and third decades of this century,
      "there are indications that his stock is slowly rising."

5   MILLGATE, MICHAEL. "Faulkner and Lanier: A Note on the name
      Jason." Mississippi Quarterly, XXV (Summer), 349–350.
         Suggests connections between Jason of The Sound and the
      Fury and the farmer Jason from Lanier's "Corn."

6   MOORE, RAYBURN S. Paul Hamilton Hayne. United States Authors
      Series no. 202. New York: Twayne, pp. 168–169.
         Examines the exchanges of letters and reciprocal critical
      comments between the poets, focusing on Lanier's essay
      "Paul H. Hayne."

1973 A BOOKS – NONE

1973 B SHORTER WRITINGS

1   ANTIPPAS, A. P. and CAROL FLAKE. "Sidney Lanier's Letters to
      Clare deGraffenreid." American Literature, XLV (May),
      182–205.

1973

These letters (1875–1880) constitute a remarkable record of Lanier as poet, scholar, musician.

2 _____. "Sidney Lanier: An Unpublished Letter to Mary Day Lanier." Maryland Historical Magazine, LXVIII (Spring), 86–88.
This 1875 note concerns the writing of "Corn."

3 BLAIR, WALTER, et al. American Literature: A Brief History. Revised edition. Glenview, Illinois: Scott, Foresman, pp. 160–161.
Surmises that Lanier found science "an unmixed good" toward which he had only "small reservations."

4 BROOKS, CLEANTH; R. W. B. LEWIS; and ROBERT PENN WARREN. "Sidney Lanier," in American Literature: the Makers and the Making. Vol. II. Edited by the authors. New York: St. Martin's Press, pp. 1715–1721.
Since Southern literature celebrates life but does not contain an inner tension, Lanier's opposition of chivalric idealism to modern materialism failed in both his attack on materialism in "The Symphony" and his praise of chivalry in "The Psalm of the West." His confusion of tone in "Corn" results in sentimentality, obscurity, and pomposity, despite the fact that the poem's "healthy regionalism" is rooted in good observation of nature.

5 KELLER, DEAN H. "Addendum to BAL: Sidney Lanier." Papers of the Bibliographical Society of America, LXVII, no. 3, 330.
Adds a setting of Lanier's "Sunset" to the list of his works set to music itemized in Blanck's Bibliography of American Literature. (See 1970.B1.)

6 REDMOND, JAMES, et al. The Year's Work in English Studies—1972. Vol. LIII. New York: Humanities Press, p. 426.
Reviews De Bellis 1972.A1, calling it "sound."

7 YOUNG, THOMAS DANIEL. "How Time Has Served Two Southern Poets: Paul Hamilton Hayne and Sidney Lanier." Southern Literary Journal, V (Fall), 101–111.
Reviews De Bellis, 1972.A1, and finds his view of Lanier "impressive and unusually convincing" in stressing the musicality of verse, especially "The Symphony."

1974 A BOOKS - NONE

1974 B SHORTER WRITINGS

1   ANTIPPAS, A. P. and CAROL FLAKE. "Sidney Lanier: Some
     Unpublished Early Manuscripts." Papers of the
     Bibliographical Society of America, LXVIII (April), 174–179.
          Of these nine manuscript poems, seven sonnets show that
     Lanier worked on his sonnet sequence "In Absence" earlier
     than had been thought.   One of these sonnets is printed for
     the first time.

2   EDWARDS, C. H., JR.   "Bibliography of Sidney Lanier, 1942–
     1973." Bulletin of Bibliography, XXXI (January–March),
     29–31.
          Lists approximately sixty items, including doctoral the-
     ses, with some annotations.   Also includes reprintings, and
     reviews of The Centennial Edition of the Works of Sidney
     Lanier.   [Inaccurate in many places.]

3   STAUFFER, DONALD BARLOW.   A Short History of American Poetry.
     New York: Dutton, pp. 123–131.
          Observes that time and circumstances placed Lanier in
     "a unique position in the history of American poetry."   Con-
     sequently, he had to rely upon himself to a great degree,
     so his rejection of like-minded experimentalist Walt Whitman
     shows Lanier seeking his own voice.   His willingness to
     trust in the sensuous quality of the sound of words promised
     an American direction, away from English poetic models.

4   THOMPSON, G. R.   Review of De Bellis's Sidney Lanier.
     American Literary Scholarship An Annual/1972.   Edited by
     J. Albert Robbins.   Durham, North Carolina: Duke
     University Press, pp. 233–234.
          Notes this "fine book" comes very close to demonstrating
     the coherencies of the symphonic form of "The Symphony," as
     well as the coherencies in the poet's style, moral vision,
     and aesthetic conception of his total work.

1975 A BOOKS - NONE

1975 B SHORTER WRITINGS

1   RUBIN, LOUIS D., JR.   "The Passion of Sidney Lanier," in his
     William Elliott Shoots a Bear: Essays on the Southern
     Literary Imagination.   Baton Rouge: Louisiana State
     University Press, pp. 107–144.

1975

Explores Lanier's life and work to show why he narrowly
missed becoming a major poet. Although he sought "a unified
visionary celebration of pure essence," at first he relied
upon bloodless poetic conventions of the genteel tradition
alien to his intense nature. "Corn" showed a new direction
through the sensuous handling of language, however; and
"The Symphony" used a controlling metaphor of music while
promoting a social polemic. But its sentimentality countered his attempt to ground its abstract protest. "The
Psalm of the West" deflected him to the "rhymed plattitudes"
of occasional verse, but his reading in older literature and
absorption in the relation of music to verse, as well as his
new positive reactions to Whitman and Emerson directed him
to his true poetic voice. That voice lay in the religious
interpretation of nature, not in social protest, the celebration of the nation, or the identity of music and poetry.
"The Marshes of Glynn" revealed that voice and proclaimed
man "a natural being rather than a social being." Rubin
speculates that had Lanier developed under Northern influences sooner he would have cut short his apprenticeship and
become a major poet. Instead, his final achievement resides
in the vigor he forced into the genteel tradition.

2 SOUCIE, GARY A. "We Can Still Save Salt Marshes of Georgia,
   Carolina." Smithsonian, V (March), 82-89.
   Describes the measures taken to protect the ecology of
   the Georgia marshes which inspired "The Marshes of Glynn."

1976 A BOOKS - NONE

1976 B SHORTER WRITINGS

1 SIMMS, L. MOODY, JR. "Walter Hines Page on Southern
   Literature." Resources for American Literary Study, VI
   (Autumn), 199-208.
   Reprints Page's previously unreprinted 1887 essay which
   urged that a Southern critic emerge who would help produce
   a resurgence of great writing in the South. Simms notes
   that "no Southern writer--with the exception of Sidney
   Lanier--seems to have had any higher artistic aims" than
   those of the major magazines, and Lanier alone conceived of
   literature as an art.

2 YOUNG, THOMAS DANIEL. Review of Rubin's William Elliott
   Shoots a Bear. Mississippi Quarterly, XXIX (Fall), 615-620.
   Notes that Rubin's argument that Lanier's views on in-
   dustrialism and their relation to art were close to those

1976

of the Agrarians (Ransom, Tate, Warren) has less cogency
than usual. Young feels that some Agrarians would disagree
with Lanier's economic views, his "sentimental, high-minded
genteel progressiveness" as well as his Victorian optimism
and emotional language.

Henry Timrod

Introduction

Henry Timrod's reputation rests almost entirely upon a slim volume of poems of 1860, some partisan war verse, and a few post-war lyrics. Acquainted with William Gilmore Simms and the men of letters who congregated at Russell's Books Store, Timrod attracted the admiration of Paul Hamilton Hayne who, when editing Russell's Magazine, made certain that Timrod had an outlet for his verse. For Hayne saw him as the first poet of a Southern movement which would rival that of the New England Renaissance. But war interfered with Hayne's dream and Timrod's development, and despite his fame as "Laureate of the Confederacy" owing to his patriotic Civil War verse, he wrote little after 1863. Personal setbacks, sickness, poverty, and deep depression brought him to an early death in 1867.

His pathetic life and romantic poetry made it inevitable that he would be remembered with dignified sentimentalism during Reconstruction in the South. It is not difficult to imagine that his life was perceived to be a lived analogy to the Lost Cause. And despite the irony of the frail nature poet being enshrined in public oratory as the "Laureate of the Confederacy," Southerners would persist in cultivating this image of him. Paul Hamilton Hayne's "Introduction" to his edition of Timrod's Poems (1873) emphasized Timrod's power of imagination and his pathos, while establishing an authoritative edition of his work. But it was the "Memorial edition" of 1899 which generated the greatest enthusiasm, perhaps because time had created a myth.

Despite the fact that Timrod's poems became venerated in the effort to memorialize his work and life, Northern critics were largely indifferent. His vitriolic battle-cry "Carolina" and his galling "Ethnogenesis" had inflicted an insult not soon forgotten. When remembered at all he was placed below Lanier and slightly above Hayne.

But unlike Hayne or Lanier, Timrod did not have a visible public life, nor did he seek to publicize himself in epistles to well-established writers, as Hayne did. His journalistic exercises with Russell's Magazine often rubbed the pompous Simms the wrong way, though they did evoke from Timrod aesthetic essays which promised a more congruent literary criticism than previously produced. Since he left no volumes of correspondence and no body of critical work, critics were frustrated in their early attempts to evaluate Timrod's development against the shaping forces of his creative consciousness. Therefore the bulk of commentary on his work was biographical. But by the end of World War I (about half of all Timrod commentary had appeared by that time), despite his gallant life, critics would detect a "self-indulgent sentimentalism." While scholars would ferret out Timrod's letters and place his life in a frame of indisputable facts, critics concerned with the art of poetry would become increasingly severe or indifferent.

By the 1940's attention turned to the construing of texts of his poetry and essays, the collecting of his minor poems, and the making of a concordance. These kinds of investigations, along with the publication of letters, continue to be the major operations of Timrod critics. Specific criticism of individual works is generally historically oriented, rather than textual. Timrod study has crested in the publications by Edd W. Parks, a biographical analysis in 1964 of Timrod, and a variorum edition of his poetry in 1965. To this date, however, none has incited more interest in Timrod and his reputation is now in decline.

Timrod is now generally understood to be a poet of lyric simplicity and patriotic fervor who imbibed the derivative sentimentalism of his section through the English romantic poets and the South's conservative literary tastes. His sentiments, as Lewisohn has observed, were virtually outmoded before he expressed them. From the point of view of modern explication techniques, his poetry lacks richness and complexity. He is therefore relegated to the position of "Poet Laureate of the Confederacy," placed second behind Lanier in the roster of nineteenth century Southern poets (excluding Poe), and studied only as an index to Southern literary developments thwarted by the Civil War.

It has been my intention to include in this reference guide of writings about Henry Timrod everything which might be of interest. But no attempt has been made to make this a complete or exhaustive bibliographical guide. However, some attempt has been made to provide a sense of Timrod's interest to historians of literature by including several histories of American writing. Items of special importance have been fully annotated to give a sense of the author's thesis and its special contribution. The index lists authors, titles, and subjects, with Timrod's works included within the index rather than under the poet's name.

Writings about
Henry Timrod, 1860–1974

1860 A BOOKS - NONE

1860 B SHORTER WRITINGS

  1   ANON. Review of The Poems of Henry Timrod. Harper's, XX
      (February), 404.
         Discovers that these poems reveal "an active and delicate
      imagination."

1867 A BOOKS - NONE

1867 B SHORTER WRITINGS

  1   ANON. "Henry Timrod." Scott's Monthly Magazine, IV
      (October), 832-833.
         After elegiac remarks about Timrod's death, reprints
      Timrod's poem to his dead son, "Our Willie."

  2   SIMMS, WILLIAM GILMORE. "The Late Henry Timrod." Southern
      Society, I (12 October), 18-19.
         Praises Timrod for his "beguiling fancy," while noting
      that he had a small but loyal audience. Notes that his
      personal purity, gracefulness and chasteness were incor-
      porated in his poetry.

1873 A BOOKS - NONE

1873 B SHORTER WRITINGS

  1   ANON. "Poems of Henry Timrod." Nation, XVI (27 February),
      151-152.
         Observes that Timrod was more restrained in his anti-
      Northern poetry than other Southerners, but no Northern war
      poets excelled him; however, readers outside South Carolina
      can ignore Timrod's war verse. Anyway, his best work had
      little to do with war, but much to do with love.

1873

2   HAYNE, PAUL HAMILTON. "Memoir of Henry Timrod," in his Poems
    of Henry Timrod. New York: Hale and Son, pp. 7-69.
        In this detailed biography Hayne explores how Timrod
    fitted into the Charleston literary coterie, his relation
    to Simms and his place in the publication of Russell's Maga-
    zine. Liberally extracting from his poems and essays,
    Hayne shows the influence of Wordsworth on his early poetry
    and asserts that a better first volume of poems than Timrod's
    1860 Poems "has seldom appeared anywhere." Timrod's essays
    showed "a thorough appreciation of his subject in all its
    phases." Maintains that Timrod's career would have been
    much improved if he had made the personal acquaintance of
    the Boston literati. His poetry contains "simplicity,
    clearness, purity, and straightforward force of...imagina-
    tion."

3   HOWELLS, WILLIAM DEAN. Review of The Poems of Henry Timrod.
    Atlantic, XXXI (April), 622-623.
        Finds Timrod's poetic genius to be "essentially medita-
    tive and tenderly lyrical." Contends that his loving poems
    to his wife are superior to his war verse.

4   STODDARD, RICHARD H. Review of The Poems of Henry Timrod.
    Aldine, VI (April), 88.
        Finds Timrod's poems "deeply touching."

5   TYLER, MOSES COIT. "The Poems of Henry Timrod." Christian
    Union, VII (19 March), 228.
        Characterizes Timrod's poetic power as "at its highest
    when awakened by the enemy of his patriotism."

1874 A BOOKS - NONE

1874 B SHORTER WRITINGS

1   ANON. Review of The Poems of Henry Timrod. Literary World,
    IV (9 January), 20.
        Agrees with other critics that Timrod's poetry is "al-
    most pre-Raphaelite in the delicious minuteness of its
    word-painting."

1876 A BOOKS

1   RIVERS, WILLIAM J. A Little Book: To Obtain Means for
    Placing a Memorial Stone Upon the Grave of the Poet, Henry
    Timrod. Charleston: privately published, 53pp.

This essay, originally a eulogy given November, 1867, stresses Timrod's courage.

1876 B SHORTER WRITINGS

1   LANIER, SIDNEY. <u>Florida</u>, in <u>The Centennial Edition of the</u>
     <u>Works of Sidney Lanier</u>. Vol. VI. Edited by Philip Graham.
     Baltimore: Johns Hopkins University Press, pp. xix-xx,
     160-161.
         In the second edition of his guidebook, Lanier regretted
     that, though spontaneous and delicate, Timrod never had
     "time to learn the mere craft of the poet--the technique
     of verse." Hayne strenuously objected to this remark in a
     letter in 1877. <u>See</u> 1945.B1.

1878 A BOOKS - NONE

1878 B SHORTER WRITINGS

1   PAGE, WALTER HINES. "Henry Timrod." <u>South Atlantic</u>, I
     (March), 359-367.
         The War of Secession was poetically true to Timrod and
     his great challenge, because his "poetic creed" was "out-
     and-out Wordsworthian."

1880 A BOOKS - NONE

1880 B SHORTER WRITINGS

1   AUSTIN, HENRY. "Henry Timrod." <u>International Review</u>, IX
     (September), 310-319.
         Compares Timrod's "melody" to Poe's, finding a "perfec-
     tion of his rhythms." He is also favorably compared to
     Shelley and Wordsworth, and found to be "more spontaneous"
     than Tennyson.

1885 A BOOKS - NONE

1885 B SHORTER WRITINGS

1   HAYNE, PAUL HAMILTON. "Ante-Bellum Charleston." <u>Southern</u>
     <u>Bivouac</u>, IV (November), 327-336.
         Discusses the ways in which Charleston provided Timrod
     with a cultural context.

1887

1887 A BOOKS - NONE

1887 B SHORTER WRITINGS

    1   HIGGINSON, THOMAS WENTWORTH. "Paul Hamilton Hayne."
           Chautauquan, VII (January), 228–232.
               Timrod had more fire, lyric force, and "a certain wealth
        of utterance," than Paul Hamilton Hayne.

    2   WHIPPLE, E. W. American Literature and Other Papers. Boston:
           Houghton Mifflin, p. 131.
               Timrod's "Ode" is the "noblest poem ever written by a
        Southern poet."

1888 A BOOKS - NONE

1888 B SHORTER WRITINGS

    1   RICHARDSON, CHARLES F. "Henry Timrod," in his American
           Literature, 1607–1885. Vol. II. New York: Putnam's,
           p. 231.
               Suggests that Timrod's "inspiration" was so vivid that
        he half–expected "the incarnate spirit of springtime to ap-
        pear in rosy flesh before him."

1892 A BOOKS - NONE

1892 B SHORTER WRITINGS

    1   TRENT, WILLIAM P. William Gilmore Simms. Boston: Houghton
           Mifflin, pp. 233–235, 295–297.
               Surmises that Timrod was irked by Simms's comments on
        poetry, since Simms wrote no poetry. Trent contends that
        Timrod was "the most finely endowed mind to be found in
        the whole South."

1894 A BOOKS - NONE

1894 B SHORTER WRITINGS

    1   PICKARD, SAMUEL T. Life and Letters of John Greenleaf
           Whittier. Vol. III. Boston: Houghton Mifflin, p. 502.
               Notes that Whittier once wrote that Timrod was first
        discovered by Whittier and claimed his friendship, despite
        Timrod's "fiery" lyrics written "against the North."

2   RUTHERFORD, MILDRED. "Henry Timrod," in her <u>A Handbook of</u>
        <u>American Literature</u>. Atlanta, Georgia: Franklin,
        pp. 376–382.
            Provides a biographical sketch. Revised: 1906.B3.

<u>1895 A BOOKS – NONE</u>

<u>1895 B SHORTER WRITINGS</u>

1   BEERS, HENRY. <u>Studies in American Letters</u>. Philadelphia:
        George W. Jacobs, p. 191.
            Contends that the war developed Timrod as a poet.

2   MANLY, LOUISE. "Henry Timrod," in her <u>Southern Literature</u>
        <u>from 1579–1895</u>. Richmond, Virginia: B. F. Johnson,
        pp. 341–343.
            Gives a biographical sketch, concluding that of all
        poets from the South "none stands higher."

<u>1897 A BOOKS – NONE</u>

<u>1897 B SHORTER WRITINGS</u>

1   ANON. "Henry Timrod," in <u>The National Cyclopaedia of American</u>
        <u>Biography</u>. Vol. VII. New York: James T. White, p. 473.
            Gives a biographical sketch.

<u>1898 A BOOKS – NONE</u>

<u>1898 B SHORTER WRITINGS</u>

1   NOBLE, CHARLES. <u>Studies in American Literature</u>. New York:
        Macmillan, pp. 266–267.
            Observes that Timrod wrote some of the best Civil War
        verse.

2   PANCOAST, HENRY S. "Henry Timrod," in his <u>An Introduction to</u>
        <u>American Literature</u>. New York: Holt, pp. 256–259.
            Detects in Timrod a more distinctly Southern atmosphere
        and a stronger note of personality than in Paul Hamilton
        Hayne's work.

3   TOOKER, L. FRANK. "Timrod the Poet." <u>Century Magazine</u>,
        XXXIII (April), 932–934.

1899

        Insists that Timrod is an American poet, not merely a
Southern versifier. Compares him to Keats. Finds Timrod
sober by contrast.

1899 A BOOKS - NONE

1899 B SHORTER WRITINGS

1   ANON. Review of The Poems of Henry Timrod (Memorial Edition).
      Churchman, LXXX (8 July), 16.
         Rates Timrod third after Poe and Lanier as a Southern
      poet.

2   AUSTIN, HENRY. "Henry Timrod." Independent, LI (20 April),
      1084-1086.
         Brief biographical-critical account.

3   BRUNS, JOHN DICKSON. "Timrod and his Poetry." Charleston
      (South Carolina) Sunday News (30 April), p. 1.
         Bruns recalls how the poems found favor with Whittier
      and Longfellow. He insists that although a fine "poet of
      war," Timrod's lyrics contained "crepuscular indefinite-
      ness."

4   BRUNS, PEIRCE [sic]. "Henry Timrod." Conservative Review, I
      (May), 263-277.
         Bruns's reviews of The Collected Poems of Henry Timrod
      (1872 and 1899) contain biographical information and ex-
      tensive quotation from the poems. Bruns's first name may
      be misspelled.

5   BRYAN, GEORGE S. "Introduction," in Poems of Henry Timrod.
      Boston: Houghton Mifflin, pp. vii-xxxviii.
         Finds that Timrod's life like his poetry had "no false
      note, no doubtful sentiment," for he had the poet's mission
      of "prophet and teacher."

6   ROSS, CHARLES H. "The New Edition of Timrod." Sewanee
      Review, VII (October), 414-420.
         Compares this "Memorial Edition" to the 1860 and 1872
      editions and faults the new edition for not using the poet's
      letters, for certain errors, for praising the war verse to
      the detriment of the nature lyrics, and for the illogical
      arrangement of the poems.

7   SALLEY, A. S., JR. "Bibliography." Southern History
      Association Publications, III (October), 274-280.

A description of four volumes of poetry as well as two dozen other items, mostly in newspapers.

8   SCHERER, JAMES A. "Henry Timrod." Lutheran Quarterly, XXIX (July), 415–420.
     Timrod's life is seen as an allegory of the South's fall.

9   SHEPHERD, HENRY E. "Henry Timrod: Literary Estimate and Bibliography." Southern History Association Publications, III (October), 267–280.
     Compares Timrod to New England poets and finds him superior for having faced adversity. See 1899.B7.

1900 A BOOKS – NONE

1900 B SHORTER WRITINGS

1   AXSON, STOCKTON. "A Southern Poet: Henry Timrod." Chautauquan, XXX (March), 573–576.
     Review of the "Memorial Edition" of Timrod's poetry which identifies him as Wordsworth's "disciple" and "worthy second to Lanier."

2   WENDELL, BARRETT. A Literary History of America. New York: Scribner's, pp. 492–495.
     Surmises that "lack of articulation" kept Timrod from greatness.

1901 A BOOKS

1   AUSTIN, HENRY. Pamphlet of the Timrod Memorial Association: Proceedings at the Unveiling of the Art Memorial, May Day, 1901. Charleston, South Carolina: privately printed, 107pp.
     Contains Austin's "Memorial Poem," Thomas Della Torre's "Address on Henry Timrod," John F. Flicken's "Address on Timrod's Ancestry," and Hamilton Mabie's "The Truest of Our Lyric Poets." These are tributes and eulogies exclusively.

2   COURTENAY, WILLIAM A. A Timrod Souvenir. Aiken, South Carolina: Palmetto Press, unpaginated.
     Contains Henry Austin's "Memorial Poem," Carl McKinley's "At Timrod's Grave" (poem), and William Courtenay's "The Promise" concerning his promise to publish Timrod's poems. The "Memorial Edition" was the result of his promise.

1901

1901 B SHORTER WRITINGS

 1   ANON. "A Southern Poet." <u>Outlook</u>, LXVIII (11 May), 107–108.
       Favorably comments on the "Memorial Edition."

 2   BOWEN, ROBERT ADGER. "Henry Timrod's Poetry." <u>Book Buyer</u>,
       XXII (June), 385–387.
       Contends that one must look to perfection only in lines
       from the poems, not in stanzas or entire works. Poverty
       never permitted the sustained labor Timrod needed. His
       longer poems are marred by "unmotived multiplication of
       verses," as in "A Vision of Poesy."

 3   ONDERDONK, JAMES L. <u>History of American Verse: 1610–1897</u>.
       Chicago: A. C. McClurg, pp. 262–263.
       Notes that the North supported Timrod during Reconstruc-
       tion despite his inflamatory war poetry.

1903 A BOOKS – NONE

1903 B SHORTER WRITINGS

 1   PAINTER, F. V. N. <u>Poets of the South</u>. New York: American
       Book, pp. 65–80, 224–226.
       Relates Timrod's misfortunes to his development of a
       concrete poetry with "themes" drawn from "the ordinary
       scenes and incidents of life."

 2   ROUTH, JAMES E., JR. "Some Fugitive Poems of Timrod."
       <u>South Atlantic Quarterly</u>, II (January), 74–77.
       Discovered along with several poems by Hayne, these con-
       stitute a slender addition to Timrod's works.

1904 A BOOKS – NONE

1904 B SHORTER WRITINGS

 1   ABERNETHY, J. W. <u>The Southern Poets: Lanier, Timrod and
       Hayne</u>. New York: Maynard, Merrill, pp. 35–52.
       "Grace, tenderness, and spontaneity" are Timrod's best
       qualities, and his sonnets his "most perfect work."

 2   TRENT, WILLIAM P. <u>A Brief History of American Literature</u>.
       New York: D. Appleton, pp. 181–182.
       Places Timrod historically, clarifying his relation to
       Simms, Hayne, and the Charleston literary scene.

1905 A BOOKS - NONE

1905 B SHORTER WRITINGS

1   MIMS, EDWIN. <u>Sidney Lanier</u>. Boston: Houghton Mifflin,
     p. 293.
        Though alert to the fact that his short life made it im-
     possible for Timrod to learn the craft of poetry, Lanier
     nevertheless ranked him with Sir Philip Sidney as a son-
     neteer.

2   TRENT, W. P. <u>Southern Writers</u>. New York: Macmillan,
     pp. 302-304.
        Emphasizes the pathetic quality of his life.

1906 A BOOKS - NONE

1906 B SHORTER WRITINGS

1   HOLLIDAY, CARL. <u>A History of Southern Literature</u>. New York:
     Neale, pp. 321-333.
        Observes that Timrod saw the wondrous in the commonplace,
     particularly in "The Cotton Boll." Such a practice resulted
     from Timrod's formulations in "A Vision of Poesy."

2   HUBNER, CHARLES W. <u>Representative Southern Poets</u>. New York:
     Neale, pp. 83-105.
        Feels Timrod is unexcelled in "depth and fervor."

3   RUTHERFORD, MILDRED L. <u>The South in History and Literature</u>.
     Atlanta, Georgia: Franklin-Turner, pp. 440-451.
        Biographical commentary with summaries of the commentary
     on Timrod by Bruns and Hayne. These inclusions constitute
     a revision of 1894.B2.

1907 A BOOKS - NONE

1907 B SHORTER WRITINGS

1   BLACKWELL, R. E. "Henry Timrod," in Edwin Alderman and Joel
     Chandler Harris, <u>Library of Southern Literature</u>. Vol. XII.
     Atlanta, Georgia: Martin and Hoyt, pp. 5391-5398.
        Compares the various editions of Timrod's work and sum-
     marizes favorable comments concerning him.

1908

1908 A BOOKS - NONE

1908 B SHORTER WRITINGS

   1   BREVARD, CAROLINE MAYS. <u>Literature of the South</u>. New York:
      Broadway, pp. 143-155.
         Attempts to elicit Timrod's "poetic creed" from some of
      his poems, concluding that a poet must seek courageously
      the "all enfolding" truth.

   2   ORGAIN, KATE A. <u>Southern Authors in Poetry and Prose</u>.
      New York: Neale, pp. 175-181.
         Finds Timrod "the finest interpreter of the feelings and
      traditions and heroism of a brave people."

   3   ROUTH, JAMES E., JR. "An Unpublished Poem of Timrod." <u>South
      Atlantic Quarterly</u>, VII (April), 177-179.
         Routh adds to the Timrod canon.

1910 A BOOKS - NONE

1910 B SHORTER WRITINGS

   1   MOSES, MONTROSE J. <u>The Literature of the South</u>. New York:
      Thomas Y. Crowell, pp. 398-409.
         Focuses on the tragic fate of Timrod and the "occasional
      compelling force of his lyric beauty." "A Vision of Poesy"
      showed Timrod's potential, not his practice. If more ad-
      venturous, he might have surpassed Sidney Lanier.

   2   ROUTH, JAMES E., JR. "The Poetry of Henry Timrod." <u>South
      Atlantic Quarterly</u>, IX (July), 267-274.
         Comparing Timrod with Sidney Lanier and Paul Hamilton
      Hayne, Routh discovers that Timrod's poetry is filled with
      platitudes, reticence and caution. His love poems resemble
      Hayne's, and his landscape poetry recalls Lanier's broader
      nature poems. But none of the passion of Timrod's nature
      poetry entered his love poems. His "visions" were "blun-
      dered into" and his war poetry was "bad poetry as poetry."

1911 A BOOKS - NONE

1911 B SHORTER WRITINGS

   1   NEWCOMER, ALPHONSO. <u>American Literature</u>. Chicago: Scott,
      Foresman, pp. 270-272.

Finds Timrod ironically remembered for war poems, though he was primarily a poet of peace.

1912 A BOOKS - NONE

1912 B SHORTER WRITINGS

1   PICKETT, LA SALLE CORBELL. Literary Hearthstones of Dixie.
        Philadelphia: Lippincott, pp. 99–122.
            Praises the "flame-born poet" in describing his life.

1913 A BOOKS - NONE

1913 B SHORTER WRITINGS

1   ANON. "Slighting Southern Literature." Literary Digest,
        XLVI (31 May), 1224–1236.
            Evaluates the claims made by a reviewer of Brander
        Matthews's Introduction to the Study of American Literature
        in which the reviewer called Southern writers superior to
        their Northern counterparts.

2   PAYNE, LEONIDAS W. "Henry Timrod," in Southern Literary
        Readings. New York: Rand McNally, pp. 144–147.
            Supplies a biographical headnote to four poems.

1915 A BOOKS

1   WAUCHOPE, GEORGE A. Henry Timrod: Man and Poet. Bulletin of
        the University of South Carolina, no. 41, Part IV (April),
        unpaginated.
            Places Timrod in the context of Charleston poets, re-
        vealing parallels between Southern and English poets.

1915 B SHORTER WRITINGS - NONE

1916 A BOOKS - NONE

1916 B SHORTER WRITINGS

1   GREEN, EDWIN. A History of the University of South Carolina.
        Columbia, South Carolina: The State Company, p. 358.
            Recalls Timrod's request that Judge Longstreet play an
        "Indian" piece on the flute for him.

1918

1918 A BOOKS - NONE

1918 B SHORTER WRITINGS

1 BOYNTON, PERCY. <u>American Poetry</u>. New York: Scribner's,
   pp. 656–658.
      Condemns Timrod as a "self-indulgent sentimentalist"
   typifying Southerners. But asserts that his poems displayed
   hope in the face of calamity; thus, he gripped life closer
   than either Poe or Lanier.

2 MIMS, EDWIN. "Poets of the Civil War, Part II: The South,"
   in <u>The Cambridge History of American Literature</u>. Edited by
   William Trent, et al. New York: Macmillan, pp. 293–295,
   passim.
      Calls Timrod "the greatest Southern poet of the Civil
   War." "Cotton Boll" shows passionate indignation and "Ethnogenesis" contains "the most felicitous expression of the
   Southern temperament."

1921 A BOOKS - NONE

1921 B SHORTER WRITINGS

1 TAPPAN, EVA MARCH. <u>A Short History of England's and America's</u>
   <u>Literature</u>. Boston: Houghton Mifflin, pp. 367–368.
      Stresses the variety of tones and the constant sincerity
   of Timrod's work.

1923 A BOOKS - NONE

1923 B SHORTER WRITINGS

1 WAUCHOPE, GEORGE ARMSTRONG. "Literary South Carolina."
   <u>Bulletin of the University of South Carolina</u>, no. 133
   (1 December), pp. 38–40.
      Surveying various friendly critics, Wauchope concludes
   that Timrod's ranking in the South as second to Poe in
   "artistic endowment" resulted from his spontaneity, close
   observation of nature, and honest passion for the old heroic
   South.

1927 A BOOKS - NONE

1927 B SHORTER WRITINGS

1   MABBOTT, THOMAS O. "Some Letters of Henry Timrod." <u>American Collector</u>, III (February), 191–195.

1928 A BOOKS

1   THOMPSON, HENRY. <u>Henry Timrod: Laureate of the Confederacy</u>. Columbia, South Carolina: The State Company, 142pp.
     Contains a selection of Timrod's poems, prose, and correspondence; and many illustrations. Gives a biography, geneology, poetic tribute, various memorials, and an essay on Timrod's poetry. Thompson proposes to acquaint South Carolinians with Timrod so he may be enshrined in their hearts; therefore, his approach is biographical, not critical. Appends a bibliography.

1928 B SHORTER WRITINGS

1   HENDRICK, BURTON J. <u>The Training of an American: The Earlier Life and Letters of Walter H. Page, 1855–1913</u>. Boston: Houghton Mifflin, pp. 325–328.
     Page found Timrod's poems "a rare delight" and declared him the best Civil War poet.

1929 A BOOKS - NONE

1929 B SHORTER WRITINGS

1   HIBBARD, ADDISON. Review of Henry Thompson's <u>Henry Timrod: Laureate of the Confederacy</u>. <u>American Literature</u>, I (May), 224–225.
     Since Thompson 1928.A1 made no real effort to examine Timrod as a writer, the book is of no real interest.

2   KREYMBORG, ALFRED. <u>Our Singing Strength</u>. New York: Coward, McCann, pp. 156–158.
     Detects restrained diction but vague imagery.

3   RUSSELL, CHARLES EDWARD. <u>An Hour of American Poetry</u>. Philadelphia: J. P. Lippincott, pp. 107–108.
     Timrod gave his life to poetry.

1931

1931 A BOOKS - NONE

1931 B SHORTER WRITINGS

   1   BLANKENSHIP, RUSSELL. <u>American Literature as an Expression of</u>
        <u>the National Mind</u>. New York: Henry Holt, pp. 238-239.
           Ironically, Timrod is known today as a nature poet,
        though his war verse dubbed him "Laureate of the Confeder-
        acy."

1932 A BOOKS - NONE

1932 B SHORTER WRITINGS

   1   LEWISOHN, LUDWIG. <u>Expression in America</u>. New York: Harper
        and Brothers, pp. 44, 79-81.
           Finds Timrod easily superior to "all his contemporaries."
        Yet he wrote in outmoded "smooth verses and Roman senti-
        ments."

   2   WYNN, WILLIAM T. "Henry Timrod," in his <u>Southern Literature</u>.
        New York: Prentice-Hall, p. 513.
           Observes in this brief biographical sketch that Timrod's
        sonnets rank with the best poets.

1933 A BOOKS - NONE

1933 B SHORTER WRITINGS

   1   VOIGT, G. P. "New Light on Timrod's 'Memorial Ode.'"
        <u>American Literature</u>, IV (January), 395-396.
           Establishes that this ode was sung at Magnolia Cemetery,
        June 16, 1866, not 1867, as Hayne recorded.

1934 A BOOKS - NONE

1934 B SHORTER WRITINGS

   1   VOIGT, G. P. "Timrod's Essays in Literary Criticism."
        <u>American Literature</u>, VI (May), 163-167.
           Stressing Timrod's essays on poetry, indicates that he
        differed from Poe by asserting that poetry was "the expres-
        sion of noble forms of power," rather than "the rhythmical
        creation of beauty."

1935 A BOOKS – NONE

1935 B SHORTER WRITINGS

1   CARDWELL, GUY A., JR. "The Date of Henry Timrod's Birth."
     American Literature, VII (May), 207–208.
         Establishes that Timrod was born in 1828, not in 1827
     as his tombstone records.

1936 A BOOKS – NONE

1936 B SHORTER WRITINGS

1   BOYNTON, PERCY. Literature and American Life. Boston:
     Ginn, pp. 574–576.
         Decides that "no one of his compeers rose to the level
     reached in 'The Cotton Boll' and 'Ethnogenesis.'"

2   HUBBELL, JAY B. "Henry Timrod," in his American Life and
     Literature. Vol. II. Washington: Harper's, p. 697.
         Reviews Timrod's life and work in this brief headnote to
     six poems.

3   McMURTRIE, DOUGLAS C. "Henry Timrod," in The Dictionary of
     American Biography. Vol. XVIII. Edited by Dumas Malone.
     New York: Scribner's, pp. 558–560.
         Examines in this biographical sketch how Timrod changed
     from a diffident poet to a man of "tremendous emotion" once
     war supplanted the "mid-century commonplaces" which had
     been his subjects. If "oversweetness" and "too-pronounced
     didacticism" typify his style, his idealism and sentiment
     typify the South.

4   PARKS, EDD WINFIELD. Southern Poets. New York: American
     Book, pp. xiii, xviii, lxv–lxix.
         Considers Timrod's critical vision of poetry to be a
     reply to Poe's. Ranks Timrod's war poems above his other
     verse. Reprinted in 1938.B2.

5   _____. "Timrod's College Days." American Literature, VIII
     (November), 294–296.
         Corrects Hayne's view that Timrod entered the University
     of Georgia in 1847. He actually entered in 1845 and left
     in 1846.

6   TAYLOR, WALTER F. A History of American Letters. Boston:
     American Book, pp. 218–220, 534–535.

1937

>   Emphasizes Timrod's poetic influences and his sources.
> Sees him dreaming of the South as a beneficent world power.
> Reprinted in 1956.B1.

1937 A BOOKS – NONE

1937 B SHORTER WRITINGS

   1   BUCK, PAUL H. <u>The Road to Reunion, 1865–1900</u>. Boston:
      Little, Brown, passim.
         Notes Timrod's "yearning for the vanquished beauty of
      the past."

1938 A BOOKS – NONE

1938 B SHORTER WRITINGS

   1   KUNITZ, STANLEY and HOWARD HAYCRAFT. <u>American Authors</u>.
      New York: H. W. Wilson, pp. 753–754.
         A brief biographical description relying on Hayne's
      "memoir."

   2   PARKS, EDD WINFIELD. <u>Segments of Southern Thought</u>. Athens:
      University of Georgia Press, pp. 59–62, 94–99, 102–104,
      123–124, 149–150, 164–165.
         Reprint of 1936.B4.

   3   PATTON, LEWIS. "An Unpublished Poem by Henry Timrod."
      <u>American Literature</u>, X (May), 222–223.
         Handwriting analysis proves that a gallant poem from the
      Bulwinkle family album is the work of Timrod, written in
      1862.

   4   TAYLOR, RUPERT. "Henry Timrod's Ancestress, Hannah Caesar."
      <u>American Literature</u>, IX (January), 419–430.
         Explores court testimony to find that there was confusion
      between Timrod's ancestress and a "person of color" of the
      same name.

   5   VOIGT, G. P. "Timrod in the Light of Newly Revealed Letters."
      <u>South Atlantic Quarterly</u>, XXXVII (July), 263–269.
         Voigt's editing of these letters reveals Timrod's dis-
      taste for teaching, his attachment to Sophie Sosnowski, and
      his dissatisfactions with poetic life.

1939 A BOOKS - NONE

1939 B SHORTER WRITINGS

1 MILES, J. TOM. "Nineteenth Century Southern Literature and
   Its Five Greatest Poets." Southern Literary Messenger, I
   (September), 598–599.
      Notes that Timrod, the "Flame-born poet," didn't describe
   nature for its own sake, but in order to teach a lesson.

1940 A BOOKS - NONE

1940 B SHORTER WRITINGS

1 FIDLER, WILLIAM. "Henry Timrod: Poet of the Confederacy."
   Southern Literary Messenger, II (October), 527–532.
      Summarizes Timrod's essays, noting scholarly work done
   upon him, and insists he deserves a wider audience.

2 _____. "Unpublished Letters of Henry Timrod." Southern
   Literary Messenger, II (October), 532–535.
      These letters recount how Timrod told Rachel Lyons in
   1861 that he was "casting about for a subject" on which to
   string his "fancies."

3 _____. "Unpublished Letters of Henry Timrod." Southern
   Literary Messenger, II (November), 605–611.
      Timrod insists in these letters (1861–1862) to Rachel
   Lyons that the poet is the true metaphysician. He includes
   one of his sonnets and speculates about why national hymns
   are difficult to write, while providing ample background
   for the composition of "Katie."

4 _____. "Unpublished Letters of Henry Timrod." Southern
   Literary Messenger, II (December), 645–651.
      Explains his attitude toward war and Wordsworth.

5 HUBBELL, JAY B. "Literary Nationalism in the Old South," in
   American Studies in Honor of William Kenneth Boyd. Edited
   by David Kelly Jack. Durham, North Carolina: Duke
   University Press, pp. 175–220.
      Stresses that the States Rights and Slavery issues gave
   impetus to a unique literature in the South. Timrod at-
   tested to the non-literary reactions of Northern readers to
   Southern writers.

1940

6   POWER, JULIA. "Henry Timrod," in her <u>Shelley in America in</u>
    <u>the Nineteenth Century</u>. Lincoln, Nebraska: University of
    Nebraska, pp. 145-146.
        Finds the influence of Shelley's <u>Alastor</u> in "A Vision of
    Poesy" and traces of "Skylark" and "Euganean Hills" in "The
    Cotton Boll."

1941 A BOOKS

1   HUBBELL, JAY B., JR. <u>The Last Years of Henry Timrod, 1864-</u>
    <u>1867</u>. Durham, North Carolina: Duke University Press,
    184pp.
        Collects letters and poems facilitating scholarly analy-
    sis of Timrod's late years. Provides chapters on "Before
    1864," "1864," "1865," "1866," "1867," and on "Uncollected
    Prose" and "Uncollected Poems." One appendix contains "The
    Late Henry Timrod" by William Gilmore Simms.

1941 B SHORTER WRITINGS

1   CARDWELL, GUY A., JR. "William Henry Timrod, the Charleston
    Volunteers, and the Defense of St. Augustine." <u>North</u>
    <u>Carolina Historical Review</u>, XVIII (January), 27-37.
        Although Timrod's father published poetry, his reportage
    was matter-of-fact.

2   HUBBELL, JAY B., JR. "Some New Letters of Constance Fenimore
    Woolson." <u>New England Quarterly</u>, XIV (December), 715-735.
        Woolson found in Timrod's poetry expressions contained
    in her own verse.

1942 A BOOKS - NONE

1942 B SHORTER WRITINGS

1   CARDWELL, GUY A., JR. "Introduction," in his <u>The Uncollected</u>
    <u>Poems of Henry Timrod</u>. Athens: University of Georgia
    Press, pp. 1-19.
        Provides a preface, introduction and notes, along with
    detailed analyses of previous Timrod editions. Gathered
    from manuscript "Autograph Relics" (1844-1855) in the
    Charleston Library, as Cardwell explains in the "Introduc-
    tion," these poems will not particularly add luster to Tim-
    rod's reputation.

2 PARKS, EDD WINFIELD. "Introduction," in his The Essays of
   Henry Timrod. Athens: University of Georgia Press,
   pp. 3-60.
       Supplies a preface, introduction, and notes to four es-
   says and the poem "A Vision of Poesy." The earliest essay
   counters Poe by insisting, as Parks explains in the "Introduction," on the ethics of art, while the others, like Poe,
   stress the craft of poetry. The poem reveals the mystical
   origin of poetry. Parks concludes that Timrod's ideas developed, but never really changed. Reprinted in 1958.B2.

1943 A BOOKS - NONE

1943 B SHORTER WRITINGS

1 EIDSON, JOHN O. Tennyson in America. Athens: University of
   Georgia Press, pp. 72-73.
       Indicates similarities between "Hark to the Shouting
   Wind" of Timrod and Tennyson's "Break, Break, Break."

1945 A BOOKS - NONE

1945 B SHORTER WRITINGS

1 GRAHAM, PHILIP. The Centennial Edition of the Works of Sidney
   Lanier. Volume VI. Baltimore, Maryland: The Johns Hopkins
   University Press, pp. xix-xx, 160-161.
       Reprinting of 1876.B1.

1947 A BOOKS - NONE

1947 B SHORTER WRITINGS

1 BROOKS, VAN WYCK. The Times of Melville and Whitman. New
   York: Dutton, passim.
       Finds Timrod had a "vigorous and penetrating critical
   mind," so he was stunned at Southern indifference to him.

2 GRIFFIN, MAX L. "Whittier and Hayne: A Record of Friendship."
   American Literature, XIX (March), 41-58.
       The poets shared a mutual admiration for Timrod.

3 SIEGLER, MILLEDGE B. "Henry Timrod and Sophie Sosnowski."
   Georgia Historical Quarterly, XXXI (September), 171-180.
       Timrod's sister brought them together in 1857. His hopes
   for marriage were recorded in "Two Portraits."

1948

1948 A BOOKS - NONE

1948 B SHORTER WRITINGS

1 BENÉT, WILLIAM ROSE. The Reader's Encyclopedia. New York:
   Crowell, p. 1126.
        A very brief biographical sketch.

2 McKEITHAN, DANIEL M. "Paul Hamilton Hayne Writes to the Grand-
   daughter of Patrick Henry." Georgia Historical Quarterly,
   XXXII (March), 22-28.
        Stressing Timrod's importance as a true Southern poet,
   Hayne compares him to Tennyson.

3 SPILLER, ROBERT E., et al. Literary History of the United
   States. Vol. III. New York: Macmillan, pp. 343-344,
   747-748.
        Places Timrod in his cultural situation and provides a
   survey of bibliographical items.

1949 A BOOKS - NONE

1949 B SHORTER WRITINGS

1 FIDLER, WILLIAM. Seven Unpublished Letters of Henry Timrod.
   Alabama Review, II (April), 139-149.
        These 1861-1863 letters to Rachel Lyons mainly record
   Timrod's inability to write because of his literary isola-
   tion and the lugubrious time of war.

2 PARKS, EDD WINFIELD. "Timrod's Concept of Dreams." South
   Atlantic Quarterly, XLVIII (October), 584-588.
        Suggests that Timrod sought intuitive revelation through
   revery, so the device of the dream emerged early in his
   work. "Dreams" (1857) indicates the way the dream unfolds
   ultimate truth.

1951 A BOOKS - NONE

1951 B SHORTER WRITINGS

1 GOHDES, CLARENCE. "Henry Timrod," in The Literature of the
   American People. Edited by Arthur H. Quinn. New York:
   Appleton-Century-Crofts, passim.
        Records that Timrod uses Poe's definition of poetry as
   "rhythmic beauty" as his own premise.

1952 A BOOKS - NONE

1952 B SHORTER WRITINGS

1   BEATTY, RICHARD; FLOYD C. WATKINS; THOMAS YOUNG; and RANDALL
STEWART. <u>The Literature of the South</u>. New York: Scott,
Foresman, pp. 720-721.
      Since Timrod's war poems gave him "unquestioned" status,
the term "Laureate of the Confederacy" is apt even now.

1954 A BOOKS - NONE

1954 B SHORTER WRITINGS

1   HUBBELL, JAY B., JR. "Henry Timrod," in <u>The South in American
Literature, 1607-1900</u>. Durham, North Carolina: Duke
University Press, pp. 466-474.
      Provides an extended biographical description with a
survey of the interaction of Timrod's life and art. Finds
Hayne's "Memoir" still the best account of the poet's life,
and indicates connections to Shelley, Wordsworth, and
Tennyson.

1956 A BOOKS - NONE

1956 B SHORTER WRITINGS

1   TAYLOR, WALTER F. <u>The Story of American Letters</u>. Chicago:
Henry Regnery, pp. 198-201.
      Reprint of 1936.B6.

1957 A BOOKS - NONE

1957 B SHORTER WRITINGS

1   POCHMANN, HENRY A. <u>German Culture in America</u>. Madison:
University of Wisconsin Press, pp. 459-460.
      Contends that passages in "A Vision of Poesy" are
reminiscent of lines in <u>Faust</u>.

1958

1958 A BOOKS - NONE

1958 B SHORTER WRITINGS

   1   PARKS, EDD W. "Henry Timrod, Traditionalist," in <u>Ante-Bellum</u>
         <u>Southern Critics</u>. Athens: University of Georgia Press,
         pp. 193–226, 316–329.
            Timrod's poems, essays, and editorials are intimately
         related to one another. Revision of two paragraphs, but
         otherwise a reprint of 1942.B2.

   2   RUBIN, LOUIS D., JR. "Henry Timrod and the Dying of the
         Light." <u>Mississippi Quarterly</u>, XI (Summer), 101–111.
            Rubin argues that in Timrod's poem "Charleston" the "jux-
         taposition of surface calm and underlying trepidity gives
         the poem a tension that makes possible the dramatic impact
         of the final, resolving stanza."

1960 A BOOKS - NONE

1960 B SHORTER WRITINGS

   1   JONES, JOSEPH, et al. "Henry Timrod," in their <u>American</u>
         <u>Literary Manuscripts</u>. Austin: University of Texas Press,
         p. 372.
            Lists libraries where manuscripts by Timrod may be
         found.

1961 A BOOKS - NONE

1961 B SHORTER WRITINGS

   1   PEARCE, ROY HARVEY. "Timrod and Lanier." <u>The Continuity of</u>
         <u>American Poetry</u>. Princeton, New Jersey: Princeton
         University Press, pp. 233–236.
            War pressure forced Timrod to learn to direct his poetry
         to a Southern audience. In the war poems Timrod, like
         Whittier and Lowell, treated "communal morality."

   2   ROBILLARD, DOUGLAS J. "Henry Timrod, John R. Thompson, and
         the Ladies of Richmond." <u>South Carolina Historical</u>
         <u>Magazine</u>, LXII (July), 129–133.
            These letters to the editor of the <u>Southern Literary</u>
         <u>Messenger</u> (1867) concern Thompson's request for a photograph
         of Timrod to be raffled at a bazaar of the "Ladies of the
         Hollywood Memorial Association of Richmond."

1962 A BOOKS – NONE

1962 B SHORTER WRITINGS

1   ROBILLARD, DOUGLAS J.   "Two Timrod Letters."   North Carolina
        Historical Review, XXXIX (Autumn), 549–553.
            Since Richard H. Stoddard, a Northern editor, had praised
        Timrod's Poems, he asked him in 1865 about the prospect of
        finding work in the North. He also asked Stoddard to con-
        sider some poems for publication.

2   WILSON, EDMUND. Patriotic Gore. New York: Oxford University
        Press, p. 469.
            Identifies "Cotton Boll", as war propaganda.

1963 A BOOKS – NONE

1963 B SHORTER WRITINGS

1   SPILLER, ROBERT, et al. Literary History of the United States.
        Bibliographical Supplement. Vol. I. Revised Third Edition.
        New York: Macmillan, p. 200.
            Lists the major works of Timrod scholarship.

1964 A BOOKS

1   PARKS, EDD WINFIELD. Henry Timrod. United States Authors
        Series, no. 53. New York: Twayne, 158pp.
            Provides a detailed biographical approach to Timrod's
        poetry, discussing his association with Charleston writers,
        the effect of the Civil War on his writing, and the sources
        and influences on his aesthetic theory and poetic practices.
        Suggests it is misleading to call Timrod "the Laureate of
        the Confederacy" since he opposed war, but he is still
        "humanly and poetically" at his best in his memorial "Ode."

1964 B SHORTER WRITINGS – NONE

1965 A BOOKS – NONE

1965 B SHORTER WRITINGS

1   ATCHISON, RAY M. "Scott's Monthly Magazine: A Georgia Post-
        Bellum Periodical of Literature and Military History."
        Georgia Historical Quarterly, XLIX (September), 294–305.

1965

>   Examines how Timrod sent four of his last poems to
> Scott's Monthly Magazine, among which were two about his
> son's death.

2   HART, JAMES D. "Henry Timrod," in The Oxford Companion to
>   American Literature. New York: Oxford University Press,
>   p. 848.
>>   Claims Timrod's best poems blend severity and pessimism.

3   PARKS, EDD WINFIELD and AILEEN WELLS PARKS. "Introduction,"
>   in their Collected Poems of Henry Timrod: A Variorum
>   Edition. Athens: University of Georgia Press, pp. 1–14,
>   142–203.
>>   Surveys in the "Introduction" Timrod's literary life,
>> showing why he virtually stopped writing after 1863. Con-
>> tains extensive scholarly notes to the poems, which have
>> been arranged chronologically for the first time. Intended
>> to be a companion volume to 1942.B1.

1966 A BOOKS - NONE

1966 B SHORTER WRITINGS

1   ANON. Review of the Parks's Collected Poems of Henry Timrod.
>   American Literature, XXXVIII (May), 271.
>>   Asserts that the editors' notes and variants "make their
>> excellent work the most essential book for the study of
>> Timrod." See 1965.B3.

2   ANON. Review of the Parks's Collected Poems of Henry Timrod.
>   Choice, III (May), 212.
>>   Decides that the editorial contribution is "exemplary,"
>> and advises colleges and universities to acquire the book.
>> See 1965.B3.

3   SPECTOR, ROBERT D. Notice of the Parks's Collected Poems of
>   Henry Timrod. Saturday Review, XLIX (19 February), 43.
>>   Compares Timrod to Poe, concluding that by contrast Poe
>> seems to be a great poet—but only by contrast to such a
>> poet as Timrod. See 1965.B3.

4   SULLIVAN, WALTER. "Affectionate Care." South Atlantic
>   Bulletin, XXXI (March), 13.
>>   Contends that although Timrod is second-rate, he deserved
>> the lavish care the editors evinced in compiling this
>> Variorum edition of Timrod's Collected Poems. See 1965.B3.

5   YOUNG, THOMAS D. Review of <u>The Collected Poems of Henry</u>
       <u>Timrod: A Variorum Edition</u>. <u>Mississippi Quarterly</u>, XIX
       (Spring), 92–99.
          Provides a systematic analysis of this edition, conclud-
       ing that it allows "anyone with sufficient interest to make
       his own evaluation" of Timrod. <u>See</u> 1965.B3.

1967 A BOOKS - NONE

1967 B SHORTER WRITINGS

1   McMICHAEL, JAMES. Review of <u>The Collected Poems of Henry</u>
       <u>Timrod: A Variorum Edition</u>. <u>Southern Review</u>, III (Spring),
       434–435.
          Suggests that Timrod still deserves attention because of
       his odd blend of a beguiling fragility and a trite chauvin-
       ism, seen best in "Charleston." <u>See</u> 1965.B3.

2   PARKS, EDD WINFIELD. "Timrod and Sims [<u>sic</u>]." <u>South Atlantic</u>
       <u>Bulletin</u>, XXXII (May), 6–7.
          Although a collected edition of Timrod is feasible, the
       bulk of Simms' work and the state of his manuscripts pro-
       hibit a collected edition of his work.

3   WAGENKNECHT, EDWARD. <u>John Greenleaf Whittier</u>. New York:
       Oxford University Press, p. 116.
          Whittier felt Timrod had "the true fire within."

1968 A BOOKS - NONE

1968 B SHORTER WRITINGS

1   EATON, CLEMENT. <u>The Waning of the Old South Civilization:</u>
       <u>1860–1880's</u>. Athens: University of Georgia Press,
       pp. 97–98.
          Places Timrod's "patriotic poetry" in its context.

2   WAGGONER, HYATT H. <u>American Poets from the Puritans to the</u>
       <u>Present</u>. Boston: Houghton Mifflin, p. 235.
          Finds Timrod's work, along with Hayne's, "so pathetic
       that to call Lanier's <u>better</u> is not to say anything abso-
       lutely positive."

1969

1969 A BOOKS - NONE

1969 B SHORTER WRITINGS

1   PARKS, EDD WINFIELD. "Henry Timrod," in A Bibliographical
     Guide to the Study of Southern Literature. Edited by
     Louis D. Rubin, Jr. Baton Rouge: Louisiana State Univer-
     sity Press, pp. 309–310.
          A highly selective checklist similar to that of Parks's
     Henry Timrod 1964.A1.

1970 A BOOKS - NONE

1970 B SHORTER WRITINGS

1   GREEN, CLAUDE B. "Henry Timrod and the South." South
     Carolina Review, II (May), 27–33.
          While Timrod's name is still tied to the label, "Laureate
     of the Confederacy," his war poems were in fact peace poems,
     since they recorded not Southern tragedy but "universal
     issues of human existence."

1972 A BOOKS - NONE

1972 B SHORTER WRITINGS

1   DE BELLIS, JACK. Sidney Lanier. Twayne United States Authors
     Series, no. 205. New York: Twayne, pp. 74–75.
          Asserts that Lanier was overhasty in criticizing Timrod
     in Florida and in his critical study of Timrod for not
     having had time to learn "the craft of the poet--the tech-
     nique of verse." See 1964.A1.

2   HUBBELL, JAY B. Who Are the Major American Writers? Durham,
     North Carolina: Duke University Press, p. 38.
          Notes that Edwin Whipple in 1876 picked Timrod's "Ode"
     "in its simple grandeur" as "the noblest poem ever written
     by a Southern poet."

3   MURPHY, CHRISTINA J. "Henry Timrod: Poet and Critic."
     Dissertation Abstracts International, XXXII (May), 6386A.
          Approaches Timrod from his view of the writer's relation
     to society, showing how forms of his poetry changed as his
     idea of the poet's role altered. With chapters on Charles-
     ton, Timrod's criticism, and his early poetry, she theorizes
     that Timrod vacilated between a belief in a purely

individual perception and a sensitivity to social problems. His best poems blend these attitudes, and thus Timrod deserves ranking with Bryant, Holmes, and Whittier.

1973 A BOOKS - NONE

1973 B SHORTER WRITINGS

1   SPILLER, ROBERT, et al. "Henry Timrod," in their <u>Literary History of the United States. Bibliographical Supplement</u>. Vol. II. New York: Macmillan, p. 267.
     Lists the half-dozen items appearing since 1963.

1974 A BOOKS - NONE

1974 B SHORTER WRITINGS

1   STAUFFER, DONALD BARLOW. <u>A Short History of American Poetry</u>. New York: E. P. Dutton, pp. 190-193.
     Argues that Timrod deserves Tennyson's epithet of "Poet Laureate of the South," rather than "Poet Laureate of the Confederacy," since his greatest poems reveal the tragedy of war and celebrate the tragic dead. Contends that Timrod's earlier lyrics and love poems compare favorably to those of Lowell, Whittier and Longfellow.

Paul Hamilton Hayne

Introduction

Paul Hamilton Hayne was a man of letters. He published several volumes of poetry, edited a major literary journal, wrote two biographies, edited the poetry of Timrod with an introductory essay on Timrod crucial to subsequent Timrod criticism, reviewed poetry and fiction, and wrote a voluminous number of letters to the important writers of his time—Lanier, Timrod, Simms, Bayard Taylor, Whittier, Longfellow, Lowell, Holmes, Tennyson and Swinburne among them.

Initial commentary on Hayne was generous. Since he labored during Reconstruction under great hardship and since he strove to earn his living purely from his pen, he was characterized by fellow Southerners as courageous and forgiving, graceful and idealizing. Such critics responded to the sentimental, romantic and optimistic in his poetry, while admiring the traditional values associated with the ante-bellum South. Later attempts to place Hayne's work historically found his poetry to be very uneven, since he wrote in out-moded traditions like narrative legend, or because he deliberately wrote poetry for certain occasions, or because he consciously tried to please the policies of various editors, North and South. His critical pieces reveal no aesthetic viewpoint except taste and moralism, and his methods of composition showed a lack of self-criticism.

By the end of the World War, with the advent of greater precision in scholarly techniques and closer analysis of the poetic text, critics turned to Hayne as a central figure in the development of Southern literature, rather than as an important poet. Attention thus focused on the compilation of his letters, the clarification of his sources and influences, the position he held with regard to the important ideas of his age, and the personal force he exerted among his contemporaries. The major pattern in Hayne criticism developing then—and continuing to this time—is, therefore, historical. As recently as 1973, Thomas Daniel Young favorably reviewed Rayburn S. Moore's book on Hayne primarily because it made no high claims for Hayne as an artist but instead chose to set him as a minor writer solidly in his historical milieu. The early designation of Hayne has thus stuck: Poet Laureate of the South.

Some critical debate has concerned itself with the formulation of the role Hayne played in his milieu. Although he seemed to have aligned himself with the Southern gentry, to which he had ancestral claims, he has been criticized for pretensions to the role of the Southern Longfellow at a time when such a pose was evasive. For the demands of the New South were apparent during Reconstruction and Hayne chose to ignore them, as Montrose Moses pointed out in 1908. Likewise, his violent attacks on Whitman and his dissmissive attitude toward Henry James and William Dean Howells showed him to be reactionary. Thus some commentators see Hayne as clutching a dream of the Southern milieu which faded in his grasp. As one critic put it, Hayne was "the last of the literary cavaliers." Modern concern with the poet seems destined to focus upon what it meant to bear that title.

Although no reference guide can claim utter completeness, I have attempted to include everything which might be of interest to the serious student. Each item bears an annotation which attempts to show what its chief argument or special importance might be. The index lists authors, titles, and subjects. Hayne's works are included in the general index, rather than under the poet's own name.

Writings about
Paul Hamilton Hayne, 1855–1974

1855 A BOOKS - NONE

1855 B SHORTER WRITINGS

1   ANON. Review of Poems. Harper's New Monthly, X (January),
    283-284.
        Praises his "fluent versification" and good images.

2   ANON. Review of Poems. Putnam's Monthly, V (February), 217.
    The poems are "an efflux of mere emotions."

3   ANON. "Hayne's Poems." Southern Literary Messenger, XX
    (February), 122-124.
        Poems are proof that the South can produce true poetry.
    Extensive quotations reveal fine, arresting images and
    resonant thoughts.

4   WHIPPLE, EDWIN. Review of Poems. Graham's Magazine, XLVII
    (February), 192-193.
        Lauds the "artistic sense" and "great promise" revealed.

1860 A BOOKS - NONE

1860 B SHORTER WRITINGS

1   LOWELL, JAMES RUSSELL. Review of Alvolio. Atlantic, V
    (January), 123-124.
        Alvolio contains a "great deal of real poetic feeling,
    thoughtfulness, culture, sensibility to natural beauty and
    great refinement of feeling."

1869

1869 A BOOKS – NONE

1869 B SHORTER WRITINGS

1   DAVIDSON, JAMES W. "Paul Hamilton Hayne," in <u>Living Writers</u>
       <u>of the South</u>. Edited by the author. New York: Carleton,
       pp. 242–250.
          Suggests that Tennyson might have written the shorter
       lyrics "without damage to his reputation."

1870 A BOOKS – NONE

1870 B SHORTER WRITINGS

1   BLEDSOE, ARTHUR. Review of Davidson's <u>Living Writers of the</u>
       <u>South</u>. <u>Southern Review</u>, VIII (July), 222–228.
          Challenges Davidson's deprecating view of the nature
       poetry.

1872 A BOOKS – NONE

1872 B SHORTER WRITINGS

1   HOWELLS, WILLIAM DEAN. Review of <u>Legends and Lyrics</u>.
       <u>Atlantic</u>, XXIX (April), 501–502.
          Finds that the South's Civil War experiences have been
       celebrated with "uncommon temperance and dignity."

2   PRESTON, MARGARET. Review of <u>Legends and Lyrics</u>. <u>Southern</u>
       <u>Magazine</u>, X:377–381.
          Exciting diversity of tone, ranging from the Chaucerian
       "Wife of Brittany" to the Lydian "Ode to Sleep." His son-
       nets match Rossetti's.

3   [STODDARD, HENRY]. Review of <u>Legends and Lyrics</u>. <u>The Aldine</u>,
       V (March), 68.
          The best Southern poet, next to Timrod, with a graceful
       sense of narrative verse.

1873 A BOOKS – NONE

1873 B SHORTER WRITINGS

1   TYLER, MOSES COIT. "The Poems of Henry Timrod." <u>The</u>
       <u>Christian Union</u>, VII (19 March), 228.

Suggests that Hayne could have improved his essay on
Timrod "by studious recasting of it."

1874 A BOOKS - NONE

1874 B SHORTER WRITINGS

1   ANON. Review of Legends and Lyrics. Literary World, IV
      (9 January), 20.
        "The Bonny Brown Hand" was typical of Hayne's "pleasant,
healthful" work.

1875 A BOOKS - NONE

1875 B SHORTER WRITINGS

1   ANON. Review of The Mountain of the Lovers. Appleton's
      Journal, XIII (26 June), 823-824.
        Asserts that Hayne is a modest poet of some descriptive
power whose short poems, written from direct experience
are better than his narrative poems which lack vigor.

2   ANON. "Poetry of the South." The Christian Union, XII
      (14 July), 28.
        Contends that these faithful pictures of nature are the
result of affectionate loyalty to the South.

3   ANON. Review of The Mountain of the Lovers. Scribner's, X
      (September), 647.
        Praises Hayne for his "melody of verse, clearness of
diction, power of stating directly and forcibly what he
wants to say."

4   ANON. Review of The Mountain of the Lovers. The Aldine, VII
      (September), 420.
        Finds Hayne's narratives "charmingly told," and is most
impressed by the "tenderly truthful" "Frieda and Her Poet,"
and the "simply perfect" "The Vengeance of the Goddess
Diana," revised from a much earlier version.

5   DUYCKINCK, EVERT and GEORGE DUYCKINCK. "Paul Hamilton Hayne,"
      in Cyclopedia of American Literature. Edited by Evert and
George Duyckinck. Philadelphia: William Rutter,
pp. 735-738.
        A biographical sketch is provided.

1875

6   HARRISON, JAMES. Review of <u>The Mountain of the Lovers</u>.
    <u>Southern Magazine</u>, XVII (September), 380–383.
       Contends that although Hayne has no striking originality,
    he does have "airy grace and tenderness." Although the long
    narratives lack grace and warmth, the short poems have "fer-
    vor in the utterance," especially in dedicatory poems like
    the memorial poem, "By the Grave of Henry Timrod."

7   HOWELLS, WILLIAM DEAN. Review of <u>The Mountain of the Lovers</u>.
    <u>Atlantic</u>, XXXVI (October), 495.
       Discovers in Hayne's poems "sly humor, easy satire,
    sympathy of nature and legend."

8   LANIER, SIDNEY. "The Poetry of Paul Hamilton Hayne."
    <u>Southern Magazine</u>, XVI (January), 40–48.
       Asserts that the poetry is "thoroughly and charmingly
    tuneful," and that the words and rhythms of "Fire Pictures"
    are "incontrovertible." Hayne's resistance to materialism
    in his use of nature and family as major subjects pleases
    Lanier, but Hayne's poetry is weakened by "trite similes
    and commonplace sentiments" creating "diffuseness." Re-
    printed in 1903.B1 and 1945.B3.

1879 A BOOKS – NONE

1879 B SHORTER WRITINGS

1   GILMAN, A., et al. "Paul Hamilton Hayne," in <u>Poets' Homes</u>.
    Edited by the author, et al. Boston: Houghton Mifflin,
    pp. 172–195.
       Describes Hayne's "pine barrens" home in Georgia in
    great detail.

1881 A BOOKS – NONE

1881 B SHORTER WRITINGS

1   WILLARD, FRANCES. "Notes of Southern Literary Men and Women."
    <u>Independent</u>, XXXIII (1 September), 4.
       Noting that Hayne was the only Southern poet to live ex-
    clusively from his writings, Hayne is cited for "exquisite
    finish, delicate, melodious, brilliant imagery, but marred
    by occasional affectations of obsolete phraseology and
    strained quaintness of expression."

1882 A BOOKS – NONE

1882 B SHORTER WRITINGS

1   DIDIER, EUGENE L. "Living American Authors: Paul Hamilton
    Hayne." <u>American</u>, III:231–233.
         Comprises a biographical summary emphasizing Hayne's
    literary activities and the wide range of subjects and
    tones in his poetry. Notes that Victor Hugo admired him.

2   PRESTON, MARGARET J. "Introduction," in <u>Complete Poems of
    Paul Hamilton Hayne</u>. Edited by the author. Boston:
    D. Lothrop, pp. v–viii.
         Views him essentially as a nature poet, after sketching
    his life and literary accomplishments.

1885 A BOOKS – NONE

1885 B SHORTER WRITINGS

1   DESHLER, CHARLES. Review of <u>Complete Poems of Paul Hamilton
    Hayne</u>. <u>Harper's</u>, LXXI (June), 156.
         Finds the poems freighted with melody and impassioned.

1886 A BOOKS – NONE

1886 B SHORTER WRITINGS

1   ANON. "Paul H. Hayne." <u>The Literary World</u>, XVII (24 July),
    249.
         A biographical obituary of the poet who died July 6.

2   HAYNE, PAUL HAMILTON. "A Poet's Letters to a Friend."
    <u>Critic</u>, VIII (13 February), 77–78.
         These letters from Sidney Lanier 1869–1880 (continued in
    1886.B3) contain much criticism of Hayne's work. Lanier
    found "Fire Pictures" a "rare flame-beauty," and "The
    Macrobian Bow" full of "dramatic verve." "Violets" could
    serve to take him to heaven. Lanier contends that Hayne's
    later verse showed "a distinct growth...higher and quieter."
    In turn, Lanier respected Hayne's evaluations of his own
    poems and acknowledged his "great encouragement." Reprinted
    in 1899.B1 and 1945.B2.

3   _____. "A Poet's Letter to a Friend." <u>Critic</u>, VIII
    (20 February), 89–90.
         <u>See</u> 1886.B2. Reprinted in 1899.B1 and 1945.B2.

1886

4 HILL, JOSEPH A. "Paul Hamilton Hayne." Independent, XXXVIII
   (19 August), 1039–1040.
      Describes Hayne's life, stressing his post–Civil War re-
   covery when he retired to "Copse Hill" and sought to live
   completely by his pen. Maintains he was a poet of purity
   and truth as well as a poet of Nature.

5 PRESTON, MARGARET J. "Paul Hamilton Hayne." Southern
   Bivouac, N. S. II (September), pp. 222–229.
      Examines the formative influences on Hayne, from his
   mother's inculcating Christian tenderness to his friendship
   with various writers in Charleston. As a Southern poet he
   was sensitive to Henry Timrod's work, and his edition of
   Timrod created Timrod's fame. In his role of poet he
   wished to become "The Poet of his Southern Land." Yet he
   may be finally remembered as a Southern Longfellow since
   they shared the same themes of Home, Hearth, and Heaven.
   As a correspondent and reviewer, he never wrote a "bitter
   judgment." He was a man "of very chivalrous and high-bred
   feeling."

1887 A BOOKS – NONE

1887 B SHORTER WRITINGS

1 HIGGINSON, THOMAS WENTWORTH. "Paul Hamilton Hayne."
   Chautauquan, VII (January), 228–232.
      Suggests that Hayne achieved a "crown of manliness more
   noble than any flights of song" because he deleted all bitterness from his work, although the literary and historical
   situation of the South inspired "fire" in its poets. Yet
   a fair estimate of his worth can only begin with an understanding of the South.

1888 A BOOKS – NONE

1888 B SHORTER WRITINGS

1 RICHARDSON, CHARLES F. "Paul Hamilton Hayne," in his American
   Literature, 1607–1885. Vol. II. New York: Putnam's,
   pp. 229–230.
      In this headnote to several Hayne poems, Richardson con-
   tends that nature, not war, was Hayne's great subject.

2 THOMPSON, MAURICE. "Paul Hamilton Hayne." Literature, I
   (22 September), 325–338.

Surveys the life of this pre-eminent Southern man of letters, regretting that so much of what he wrote was written for money and should therefore be excised from his complete poems. Finds the best work a mixture of Southern "sights" and English "thoughts." He excelled at the sonnet--its spirit if not its form.

1890 A BOOKS - NONE

1890 B SHORTER WRITINGS

1 BOWEN, JOHN E. "A Brief Correspondence with Paul Hamilton Hayne." Lippincott's Magazine, XLVI (September), 368-374.
In these 1886 letters to this poetry editor, Hayne confides his admiration of Swinburne, his revisions of a sonnet to Tennyson, and his fear of dying.

2 SLADEN, DOUGLAS. "Some Younger American Poets." Independent, XLII (12 June), 806.
Calls him the patriarch of the young poets, who, though uneven, produced vivid, eloquent poems.

1892 A BOOKS - NONE

1892 B SHORTER WRITINGS

1 HAYNE, WILLIAM H. "Paul Hamilton Hayne's Methods of Composition." Lippincott's Magazine, L (December), 793-796.
Emphasizes his father's "nerve-force" in revising, his inspirational meditative walks, and his spontaneity. See Parks (1936.B5), pp. 353-354 for an extract. See also 1970.B1.

2 TRENT, WILLIAM P. William Gilmore Simms. Boston: Houghton Mifflin, pp. 228-232, 275-279, 311-314, 316-318.
Except for Simms, Hayne is "the noblest and most charming character" among Southern writers. Quotes extensively from letters now lost. Though he lacked Simms' vigor or Timrod's artistic control, he was more keenly alive to nature than either.

1894

1894 A BOOKS - NONE

1894 B SHORTER WRITINGS

   1   LINK, S. A. "Sidney Lanier." <u>New England Magazine</u> (Boston),
        N. S. X (March), pp. 14–19.
           Suggests that "no other poet of his region has produced
        so much good poetry," as Hayne.

   2   PICKARD, SAMUEL T. <u>Life and Letters of John Greenleaf</u>
        <u>Whittier</u>. Vol. II. Boston: Houghton Mifflin, pp. 501–502.
           Asserts that Hayne's poems about Whittier provide "one
        of the best pictures of Whittier in his home life."

   3   WALTON, JOSEPHINE. "Sidney Lanier," in <u>American Literature</u>.
        Edited by Mildred Rutherford. Atlanta, Georgia:
        Franklin, pp. 360–367.
           Finds Hayne deserving of his title "Laureate of the
        South" because of his vast contribution to Southern literary
        impulses. Summarizes various favorable critical comments
        on Hayne. Reprinted in 1906.B4.

1895 A BOOKS - NONE

1895 B SHORTER WRITINGS

   1   MANLY, LOUISE. <u>Southern Literature from 1579–1895</u>. Richmond,
        Virginia: B. F. Johnson, pp. 346–350.
           Provides a general biographical sketch.

1896 A BOOKS - NONE

1896 B SHORTER WRITINGS

   1   PATTEE, FRED LEWIS. <u>A History of American Literature</u>.
        New York: Silver, Burdett, pp. 386–388.
           Surmises that as a student of nature and observer of the
        family, "Hayne did for the South what Whittier did for the
        North." Detects that Hayne was of the "imaginative school"
        of lyricists, whose craftsmanship is best seen in his
        sonnets.

1897 A BOOKS - NONE

1897 B SHORTER WRITINGS

1   ANON. "Paul Hamilton Hayne." The National Cyclopedia of
        American Biography. Vol. IV. New York: James T. White,
        pp. 307-308.
            Offers a short biographical sketch with illustration.

1898 A BOOKS - NONE

1898 B SHORTER WRITINGS

1   NOBLE, CHARLES. Studies in American Literature. New York:
        Macmillan, p. 268.
            Illustrates the "earnest, pure character" of Hayne's
        thought with his poem "Fate, or God?"

2   PANCOAST, HENRY S. An Introduction to American Literature.
        New York: Henry Holt, pp. 256-259.
            Stresses the similarities between Hayne and William
        Morris and Lehigh Hunt in Hayne's feeling for "classic and
        romantic ideals."

1899 A BOOKS - NONE

1899 B SHORTER WRITINGS

1   HAYNE, PAUL HAMILTON. "A Poet's Letters to a Friend," in
        The Letters of Sidney Lanier. Edited by Henry Wysham
        Lanier. New York: Scribner's, pp. 219-245.
            Reprint of 1886.B2, B3. Reprinted in 1945.B2, B3.

2   LINK, SAMUEL. Pioneers of Southern Literature. Nashville,
        Tennessee: M. E. Church, pp. 43-89.
            Contends that Hayne earned by "divine right" his title
        "Poet Laureate of the South." Thus Hayne is very critical
        of the South's disregard of him.

3   MORSE, JOHN T. Life and Letters of Oliver Wendell Holmes.
        Vol. I. Boston: Houghton Mifflin, p. 329.
            Holmes approves Hayne's proffered sonnet and sends it
        to the editors of Old and New in 1870.

1900

1900 A BOOKS - NONE

1900 B SHORTER WRITINGS

1   BATES, KATHARINE LEE. American Literature. New York:
     Macmillan, pp. 187–188.
         Suggests that Hayne's writing was his consolation for
     losses suffered during the Civil War.

1901 A BOOKS - NONE

1901 B SHORTER WRITINGS

1   ONDERDONK, JAMES L. History of American Verse: 1610–1897.
     Chicago: A. C. McClurg, pp. 186–187.
         A better term for Hayne than "Laureate of the Confeder-
     acy" would be "Woodland Minstrel of the South."

2   THOMPSON, MAURICE. "The Last Literary Cavalier." Critic,
     XXXVIII (April), 353–354.
         Hayne stood "for the best and farthest reach of art per-
     missible under the regime of slavery." Hayne did not real-
     ize that art needed absolute freedom to really thrive.
     Thompson found Hayne, the "end of an era," living in sad
     circumstances when he visited his home, the "Copse," in
     1881. Hayne was puzzled by his eclipse by Lanier.

1902 A BOOKS - NONE

1902 B SHORTER WRITINGS

1   HIGGINSON, THOMAS WENTWORTH. John Greenleaf Whittier.
     New York: Macmillan, pp. 113–114.
         Hayne's poems offer the best view of Whittier's homelife.

2   MABIE, HAMILTON W. "The Poetry of the South." International
     Monthly, V (February), 201–223.
         Lacking Timrod's power, he yet had a vivid imagination
     and perfect sincerity in treating the Old South.

1903 A BOOKS - NONE

1903 B SHORTER WRITINGS

1   LANIER, SIDNEY. "Paul H. Hayne's Poetry," in <u>Music and</u>
<u>Poetry</u>. Edited by Henry W. Lanier. New York: Scribner's,
pp. 197-211.
      Reprint of 1875.B8.

2   PAINTER, F. V. N. <u>Poets of the South</u>. New York: American
Book, pp. 221-223.
      Detects a "singular delicacy of sentiment and expres-
sion" in Hayne, "the prince of sonneteers."

1904 A BOOKS - NONE

1904 B SHORTER WRITINGS

1   ABERNETHY, J. W. <u>The Southern Poets: Lanier, Timrod, Hayne</u>.
New York: Maynard, Merrill, pp. 553-562.
      Because of Hayne's "tender regret for the irrevocable
past," he is aptly dubbed "the Poet Laureate of the South."
His chief fault is his diffuseness related to his "melodi-
ous description."

1905 A BOOKS - NONE

1905 B SHORTER WRITINGS

1   MIMS, EDWIN. <u>Sidney Lanier</u>. Boston: Houghton Mifflin,
pp. 289-292.
      Hayne insisted that the South apply a critical attitude
toward its writing. Lanier's essay on Hayne (<u>see</u> 1903.B1)
turned this critical eye on him and, though even-handed,
was not well received by Hayne.

2   TRENT, WILLIAM P. <u>Southern Writers</u>. New York: Macmillan,
pp. 318-319.
      Concludes this biographical sketch by asserting that "no
other Southern writer has displayed a more delicately re-
ceptive genius."

3   WENDELL, BARRETT. <u>A Literary History of America</u>. New York:
Scribner's, pp. 490-492.
      Finds that Hayne lacked the passion of Timrod or Lanier,
although he was in sympathy with "traditions of the South

1906

> Carolina gentry." Asserts that some of his most praised
> poetry is too imitative, while his essay on Timrod is so
> "florid" in its praise it overpowers Timrod's verse.

1906 A BOOKS - NONE

1906 B SHORTER WRITINGS

    1   BROWN, J. THOMPSON, JR. "Paul Hamilton Hayne." Sewanee
        Review, XIV (April), 236–247.
           Suggests that this "priest of nature" shows "moving
        power" in his nature lyrics.

    2   HOLLIDAY, CARL. A History of Southern Literature. New York:
        Neale, pp. 334–343.
           Argues that Hayne "told simply what he felt, and, because
        he felt intensely, he was effective in communicating his
        emotions." Lacking in Timrod's vigor, he was more dis-
        criminating than Timrod as a "lover of special forms of
        nature."

    3   HUBNER, CHARLES W. Representative Southern Poets. New York:
        Neale, pp. 55–82.
           Supplies a context for Hayne's poem about Hubner's
        daughter, "A Child's Horoscope," by quoting extensively
        from Hayne's letters to him.

    4   RUTHERFORD, MILDRED L. The South in History and Literature.
        Athens, Georgia: Franklin-Turner, pp. 452–462.
           Reprint of 1894.B3.

    5   TRAUBEL, HORACE. With Walt Whitman in Camden. Vol. II.
        Boston: Small, Maynard, p. 476.
           Whitman called Hayne one of the few good love poets in
        America.

1907 A BOOKS - NONE

1907 B SHORTER WRITINGS

    1   MIMS, EDWIN. "Paul Hamilton Hayne," in The Library of
        Southern Literature. Vol. V. Edited by Alderman, Harris
        and Kent. New Orleans, Louisiana: Martin and Hoyt,
        pp. 2265–2271.
           Concludes that Hayne wrote distinctively Southern poetry,
        after comparing him to Simms.

1908 A BOOKS - NONE

1908 B SHORTER WRITINGS

1   BREVARD, CAROLINE MAYS. <u>Literature of the South</u>. New York:
     Broadway, pp. 156–168.
         A general review of Hayne's work.

2   HOLLIDAY, CARL. <u>Three Centuries of Southern Poetry, 1607–
     1907</u>. Nashville: M. E. Church, pp. 152–158.
         Provides biographical notes on six poems.

3   ORGAIN, KATE A. <u>Southern Authors in Poetry and Prose</u>.
     New York: Neale, pp. 63–73.
         Interweaves Hayne's poems into biographical sketch.

1910 A BOOKS - NONE

1910 B SHORTER WRITINGS

1   MOSES, MONTROSE J. <u>The Literature of the South</u>. New York:
     Thomas Y. Crowell, pp. 384–397.
         Comparing Hayne to Lanier reveals that Hayne could not
     have been a major writer in the New South. He lacked both
     "the highest imaginative quality" in his vision and "com-
     pression" in his art. This is shown in his legends and
     lyrics which lack the needed "moral consciousness" of the
     New South. Despite his wide correspondence with other
     writers, Hayne "shut his ear to the sound of any forward
     tread."

2   ROUTH, JAMES C., JR. "Some Fugitive Poems of Paul Hamilton
     Hayne." <u>South Atlantic Quarterly</u>, IX (October), 327–333.
         Although discovered several years earlier, these seven
     poems were withheld from publication because of the "vio-
     lent sectional feeling" in three of the Civil War period.
     Routh traces their declamatory style to Byron, though they
     lack coherence. Among the other poems is a Timrodian love
     sonnet and a "machine-made" war tribute to the "Merrimac."
     <u>See</u> 1918.B3.

3   _____. "The Poetry of Henry Timrod." <u>South Atlantic
     Quarterly</u>, IX (July), 267–274.
         Observes that Hayne's love poems resembled Timrod's,
     though Timrod had more poetic daring.

1910

4   STEDMAN, LAURA and GEORGE M. GOULD. <u>The Life and Letters of</u>
     <u>Edmund Clarence Stedman</u>. Vol. I. New York: Moffat, Yard,
     pp. 505–506.
          Indicates that Hayne flattered Stedman with praise of
     his Greek translations and his critiques of Victorian poets,
     as well as his narrative poems.

<u>1911 A BOOKS – NONE</u>

<u>1911 B SHORTER WRITINGS</u>

1   NEWCOMER, ALPHONSO G. <u>American Literature</u>. Chicago: Scott,
     Foresman, pp. 270–272.
          Comparison between Hayne and Timrod reveals that Hayne
     was inferior in martial verse but superior in nature lyrics.

<u>1912 A BOOKS – NONE</u>

<u>1912 B SHORTER WRITINGS</u>

1   PICKETT, LA SALLE CORBELL. <u>Literary Hearthstones of Dixie</u>.
     Philadelphia: J. B. Lippincott, pp. 69–96.
          Recounts the tale of a ghost attached to the Hayne
     family and other basic facts about his family.

<u>1913 A BOOKS – NONE</u>

<u>1913 B SHORTER WRITINGS</u>

1   ANON. "Slighting Southern Literature." <u>Literary Digest</u>,
     XLVI (31 May), 1224–1236.
          Challenges a reviewer of Brander Matthews' <u>Introduction</u>
     <u>to the Study of American Literature</u> who called Southern
     writers superior to Northern ones.

2   HAYNE, WILLIAM H. "Some Unpublished Letters of Wilkie
     Collins." <u>Bookman</u>, XXVII (March), 66–71.
          This cordial correspondence (1884–1885), prompted by
     Hayne, elicited Collins' reflections on the decline of fic-
     tion, his fear of piracies of his work, and his worry over
     his health. Helping to place Hayne's poems, he found his
     volume made him "feel" and offered no obstacles to under-
     standing. He was deeply touched by Hayne's poem about him.

1918 A BOOKS - NONE

1918 B SHORTER WRITINGS

1   BOYNTON, PERCY. <u>American Poetry</u>. New York: Scribner's,
     pp. 659-661.
         Better as a literary journalist than a poet, he was a
     "real representative of a period and locality."

2   MIMS, EDWIN. "Poets of the Civil War: II: The South," in
     <u>The Cambridge History of American Literature</u>. Edited by
     W. P. Trent, et al. New York: Macmillan, pp. 292-293.
         The most promising writer of the Charleston group clus-
     tered around Simms; he was the first Southern poet who
     wrote with a passion, rather than as a pastime.

3   ROUTH, JAMES C., JR. "Two Fugitive Poems of Paul Hamilton
     Hayne." <u>Journal of English and German Philology</u>, XVII
     (July), 426-429.
         "Poem of the War" and "The Kentucky Partisan" were un-
     accountably not printed with other poems with which they
     were found. <u>See</u> 1910.B2.

1921 A BOOKS - NONE

1921 B SHORTER WRITINGS

1   ANON. "Five Letters from Paul Hamilton Hayne to Horatio
     Woodman." <u>Proceedings of the Massachusetts Historical
     Society</u>, LIV (January), 178-184.
         In these letters 1854-1860 Hayne dreams of going to Bos-
     ton, recounts a hunting trip to Florida, cites journals
     favorable or opposed to his work, describes the problems of
     the serious writer in provincial Charleston and declares
     himself opposed to literary sectionalism.

1923 A BOOKS - NONE

1923 B SHORTER WRITINGS

1   WAUCHOPE, GEORGE ARMSTRONG. "Literary South Carolina."
     <u>Bulletin of the University of South Carolina</u>, no. 133
     (1 December), pp. 40-41.
         Proclaims Hayne the finest sonneteer in America, notes
     his preference for the nature lyrics, and confesses to
     being deeply moved by "In Harbor."

1925

1925 A BOOKS - NONE

1925 B SHORTER WRITINGS

   1   BERNBAUM, ERNEST. "Richard Doddridge Blackmore and American
         Cordiality." <u>Southwest Review</u>, XI (October), 46-58.
            Comments on the friendly correspondence between the Eng-
         lish novelist and the Southern poet. Hayne recounted his
         literary connections to the New England writers and extended
         his hospitality to Blackmore.

1928 A BOOKS - NONE

1928 B SHORTER WRITINGS

   1   THOMPSON, HENRY. <u>Henry Timrod: Laureate of the Confederacy</u>.
         Columbia, South Carolina: The State Company, 147pp.
            Traces the Hayne-Timrod relation, especially concerning
         his publication of Timrod's poems, through the poets'
         correspondence.

1929 A BOOKS - NONE

1929 B SHORTER WRITINGS

   1   KREYMBORG, ALFRED. <u>Our Singing Strength</u>. New York: Coward
         McCann, p. 156.
            Hayne "reconstructed" ties between North and South.

   2   RUSSELL, CHARLES EDWARD. <u>An Hour of American Poetry</u>.
         Philadelphia: J. B. Lippincott, pp. 108-109.
            Hayne was an outstanding sonneteer with poetic vision.

   3   STARKE, AUBREY H. "Sidney Lanier and Paul Hamilton Hayne:
         Three Unpublished Letters." <u>American Literature</u>, I
         (March), 32-39.
            The letters reveal the "intimate relation" of the poets
         during thirteen years, especially as they sought to cling
         to the South at a time when the region was unconducive to
         men of letters.

1931 A BOOKS - NONE

1931 B SHORTER WRITINGS

1   BLANKENSHIP, RUSSELL. <u>American Literature as an Expression of</u>
     <u>the National Mind</u>. New York: Henry Holt, p. 238.
         While similar to Wordsworth, Hayne is "easier to read
     than discuss."

1932 A BOOKS - NONE

1932 B SHORTER WRITINGS

1   GORDON, ARMISTEAD C., JR. "Paul Hamilton Hayne." <u>Dictionary</u>
     <u>of American Biography</u>. Vol. VIII. New York: Scribner's,
     pp. 455–456.
         Though he "blue-penciled too seldom," Hayne deserves to
     be better known; for, although lacking "depth of thought or
     imaginative reach," he was "strong in spiritual sweetness."

2   HENCH, ATCHESON L. "Three Letters to the Haynes from Richard
     Blackmore." <u>American Literature</u>, IV (May), 199–207.
         Blackmore helped defray the cost of a church built near
     Hayne's home as a funeral monument.

3   LEWISOHN, LUDWIG. <u>Expression in America</u>. New York: Harper
     and Brothers, p. 82.
         Observes that unlike Timrod, Hayne moved away from Ten-
     nyson's influence, though he had nothing to "<u>say</u>."

4   SHAW, HARRY, JR. "Paul Hamilton Hayne to Richard Henry
     Stoddard, July 1, 1866." <u>American Literature</u>, IV (May),
     195–199.
         Recounts how Hayne sought help from Stoddard in placing
     his poems in Northern magazines.

5   WYNN, WILLIAM T. "Paul Hamilton Hayne," in his <u>Southern</u>
     <u>Literature</u>. New York: Prentice-Hall, pp. 468–469.
         Offers a brief biography with emphasis on Hayne's
     Southernness.

1933 A BOOKS - NONE

1933 B SHORTER WRITINGS

1   HUBBELL, JAY B. "George Henry Boker, Paul Hamilton Hayne, and
     Charles Warren Stoddard, Some Unpublished Letters."

1933

American Literature, V (May), 146–165.
 Written in 1867–1869, two of these letters to Hayne concern attempts to publish in Northern magazines.

2 MORDELL, ALBERT. Quaker Militant: John Greenleaf Whittier.
 Boston: Houghton Mifflin, pp. 281–283.
 Whittier had a closer relation to Hayne than to any of
the New England poets. They were "genteel and respectable
bards" despite their differences over slavery.

1934 A BOOKS – NONE

1934 B SHORTER WRITINGS

1 FERGUSON, J. DE LANCEY. "A New Letter of Paul Hamilton Hayne."
 American Literature, V (January), 368–370.
 This 1873 letter reveals Hayne accepting Howells' invi-
tation to meet that summer.

1936 A BOOKS – NONE

1936 B SHORTER WRITINGS

1 BERNARD, EDWARD G. "Northern Bryant and Southern Hayne."
 Colophon, I (Spring), 536–540.
 Concerns friendly letters 1870–1878 about Hayne's "Ode"
to William Gilmore Simms which Bryant published in 1878.

2 BOYNTON, PERCY H. Literature and American Life. Boston:
 Ginn, pp. 576–577.
 Finds that Hayne lacked gifts "to match his devotion" to
poetry, and that he was only an occasional poet "without
any special lightness, depth or felicity."

3 HARTWICK, HARRY. "Bibliography," in A History of American
 Letters. Edited by Walter F. Taylor. Boston: American
 Book, pp. 617–618.
 Lists primary and secondary items on Hayne through 1934.

4 HUBBELL, JAY B. "Paul Hamilton Hayne," in his American Life
 in Literature. Vol. II. Washington: Harper and Brothers,
 p. 697.
 Suggests in this headnote to six poems that Hayne's life
might be compared with that of Emily Dickinson.

5 PARKS, EDD WINFIELD. Southern Poets. New York: American
 Book, pp. cv–cviii, cxii–cxiii, 125–136.

Sees his work as "diffuse," concluding that Hayne never ripened, only mellowed. Yet Hayne's introduction to the poetry of Timrod is "one of the noblest" and most "penetrating" essays ever written. Reprinted in 1938.B4.

1937 A BOOKS - NONE

1937 B SHORTER WRITINGS

1 BUCK, PAUL H. The Road to Reunion, 1865–1900. Boston:
      Little, Brown, pp. 199–200.
         Briefly considers Hayne's impressions on Northern poets.

2 McKEITHAN, DANIEL M. "Paul Hamilton Hayne and The Southern
      Bivouac." University of Texas Studies in English, XVII
      (July), 112–123.
         Summarizes four essays of Hayne's from The Southern
      Bivouac, concerning Confederate War Songs, Ante-Bellum
      Charleston, the defense of Fort Wagner, and Charles Gayarré.

1938 A BOOKS - NONE

1938 B SHORTER WRITINGS

1 HOOLE, WILLIAM S. "Seven Unpublished Letters of Paul
      Hamilton Hayne." Georgia Historical Quarterly, XXII
      (September), 273–285.
         These letters concern Hayne's inquiry into his ancestry.

2 KUNITZ, STANLEY and HOWARD HAYCRAFT. American Authors, 1600–
      1900. New York: H. W. Wilson, pp. 351–352.
         Provides a biographical sketch.

3 McKEITHAN, DANIEL M. "Paul Hamilton Hayne's Reputation in
      Augusta at the Time of His Death." Studies in English,
      no. 3826 (8 July), pp. 163–173.
         Maintains that while Hayne was lionized by uncritical
      admirers, he was homesick for Charleston.

4 PARKS, EDD W. Segments of Southern Thought. Athens:
      University of Georgia Press, pp. 96–98, 103–104.
         Claims that despite his concern for nature, Hayne "never
      seems to have acquired a feeling of the richness and fertil-
      ity of earth, or of man's dependence on it." Reprint of
      1936.B5.

1939

1939 A BOOKS – NONE

1939 B SHORTER WRITINGS

    1   COLEMAN, RUFUS A. "Hayne Writes to Trowbridge." <u>American</u>
        <u>Literature</u>, X (January), 483–486.
            In this letter of 1869 Hayne proposed to submit a tale
        to Trowbridge's <u>Our Young Folks</u>.

    2   McKEITHAN, DANIEL M. "An Unpublished Poem of Paul Hamilton
        Hayne." <u>Southern Literary Messenger</u>, I (September),
        591–592.
            Reproduces a poem on the flyleaf of <u>The Diary Reminis-</u>
        <u>cences, and Correspondence of Henry Crabbe Robinson</u> (1879).
        The two quatrains concerning the theme of wisdom through
        suffering were intended for an old schoolmate and Charles-
        ton lawyer.

    3   MILES, J. TOM. "Nineteenth Century Southern Literature and
        Its Five Great Poets." <u>Southern Literary Messenger</u>, I
        (September), 597–598.
            Offers a biographical view of Hayne which finds him a
        democratic, meditative poet, unsurpassed at sonnets.

1940 A BOOKS – NONE

1940 B SHORTER WRITINGS

    1   ANDERSON, CHARLES R. "Charles Gayarré and Paul Hayne: The
        Last Literary Cavaliers," in <u>Studies in Honor of William</u>
        <u>Kenneth Boyd</u>. Edited by David K. Jackson. Durham, North
        Carolina: Duke University Press, pp. 221–281.
            These "cavaliers" were united against George W. Cable's
        views on Negro equality and they helped to block Cable's
        writing of a book on William Gilmore Simms. They resented
        the developing realism which Cable represented to them.
        Anderson bases these inferences on over one hundred letters
        written between 1885 and 1886 by Hayne and Gayarré.

    2   McKEITHAN, DANIEL M. "A Note on Hayne's Ancestry." <u>Georgia</u>
        <u>Historical Quarterly</u>, XXIV (June), 166–167.
            Quoting an unpublished letter of 1879, examines Hayne's
        paternal ancestry.

1941 A BOOKS - NONE

1941 B SHORTER WRITINGS

1 HUBBELL, JAY B. The Last Years of Henry Timrod. Durham,
       North Carolina: Duke University Press, passim.
          Presents many letters from Hayne to Timrod and Timrod to
       Hayne concerning Timrod's life and career.

2 _____. "Some New Letters of Constance Fenimore Woolson."
       New England Quarterly, XIV (December), 715-735.
          A novelist, this grandniece of James Fenimore Cooper was
       the first post-bellum Northern writer to treat the South
       sympathetically. These letters (1875-1880) reveal that
       Timrod was her "soul mate" and that she took Hayne's poetry
       on meditative walks.

1942 A BOOKS - NONE

1942 B SHORTER WRITINGS

1 CARDWELL, GUY A., JR. "Introduction," in The Uncollected
       Poems of Henry Timrod. Edited by the author. Athens:
       University of Georgia Press, pp. 1-20.
          Describes Hayne's editing of The Poems of Henry Timrod
       (1873). Since he used the proofsheets Timrod prepared in
       1864 and made judicious decisions everywhere, "one may
       safely assume...that the Hayne text is a good one."

2 McKEITHAN, DANIEL M. "A Correspondence Journal of Paul
       Hamilton Hayne." Georgia Historical Quarterly, XXVII
       (September-December), 249-272.
          Records the personal and business letters (1880-1882).

1944 A BOOKS

1 McKEITHAN, DANIEL M. A Collection of Hayne Letters. Austin:
       University of Texas Press, 499pp.
          These 245 letters are arranged by library groups, with
       an itemized list in the "Content." Since Hayne corresponded
       with dozens of significant men of letters (Lanier, Simms,
       Longfellow, Whittier, Lowell, Harris, Taylor, Holmes, Ten-
       nyson, Swinburne, Stedman and Stoddard among them) they
       reveal myriad facets of his time, of aesthetic problems in
       the nineteenth century, and of his own life. He thanks
       Lowell for reviewing his poetry and describes various

1944

projected writings. He seeks Whittier's advice about a
poem he is revising. He sends Longfellow a flattering poem
while discussing with Simms the evils of "mobocracy". To
everyone he explains his tactics for living purely by his
writing, and this enables him to tell Moses Coit Tyler of
the resistance within his culture to serious writers. He
encourages the writing of Stedman and Stoddard, while re-
ceiving great support from John James about the possible
publication of his collected poetry. McKeithan provides
extensive, detailed notes.

1944 B SHORTER WRITINGS

1   McKEITHAN, DANIEL M. Communication to the Editor in reply to
a review of his A Collection of Hayne Letters. Journal of
Southern History, X (November), 498–499.
In reply to R. C. Beatty's review, McKeithan stresses
that he was mistakenly accused of incompleteness when he
had no intention of producing a complete collection of letters. He reviews the current work-in-progress on Hayne
and surveys various groups possessing Hayne material. He
disagrees with Beatty about Hayne's view of Charleston,
insisting Hayne loved it.

1945 A BOOKS

1   DUFFY, CHARLES. The Correspondence of Bayard Taylor and Paul
Hamilton Hayne. Baton Rouge: Louisiana State University
Press, 111pp.
Duffy has edited forty-six letters, twenty-seven of
which are by Hayne. They reveal the Reconstruction milieu
in its social and literary aspects, North and South. Although they never met, Hayne and Taylor exchanged literary
gossip about Simms, Lanier, and Whitman, among others.

1945 B SHORTER WRITINGS

1   HAYNE, PAUL HAMILTON. Defense of Henry Timrod, in The
Centennial Edition of the Works of Sidney Lanier. Vol. VI.
Edited by Philip Graham. Baltimore: Johns Hopkins
University Press, pp. xix-xx, 160–161.
Hayne vigorously objects to critical remarks on Henry
Timrod which Lanier included in his second edition of
Florida (1876). Lanier stated that Timrod "never had time
to learn...the technique of verse." Hayne replied in 1877:

"I don't believe the...American has ever existed, whose
knowledge of the 'technique of verse' surpassed Timrod's."

2   LANIER, SIDNEY. Letters to Paul Hamilton Hayne, in The
     Centennial Edition of the Works of Sidney Lanier. Vols.
     VII-X. Edited by Charles Anderson and Aubrey Starke.
     Baltimore: Johns Hopkins University Press, passim.
          Reprints 1886.B2, B3 and 1899.B1.

3   _____. "Paul H. Hayne's Poetry," in The Centennial Edition of
     the Works of Sidney Lanier. Vol. V. Edited by Garland
     Greever. Baltimore: Johns Hopkins University Press,
     322-333.
          Reprint of 1875.B8. See also 1903.B1.

1946 A BOOKS - NONE

1946 B SHORTER WRITINGS

1   McKEITHAN, DANIEL M. Selected Letters: John Garland James to
     Paul Hamilton Hayne and Mary Middleton Michel Hayne.
     Austin: University of Texas Press, pp. vii-xiii.
          These letters of 1877-1887 mainly concern Hayne's at-
     tempt to help James collect selections for his Southern
     Student's Handbook of Selections for Reading and Oratory.
     They also show how James was instrumental in the publica-
     tion in 1882 of The Complete Poems of Paul Hamilton Hayne.

2   TODD, AUBREY C. Review of Duffy's Correspondence of Bayard
     Taylor and Paul Hamilton Hayne. Southern Packet, II
     (February), 3.
          Lauds the letters for containing new biographical facts,
     evidence of Hayne's plight during Reconstruction, and
     abundant information about Hayne's literary contacts. See
     1945.A1.

1947 A BOOKS - NONE

1947 B SHORTER WRITINGS

1   ANDERSON, CHARLES R. "Poet of the Pine Barrens." Georgia
     Review, I (Fall), 280-293.
          Lanier and Hayne re-inforced one another's sense that
     the South was the best milieu for their talents and for the
     subjects of their poems. Relies upon their voluminous cor-
     respondence, 1868-1880.

1947

2 BROOKS, VAN WYCK. <u>The Times of Melville and Whitman</u>.
   New York: Dutton, passim.
        Records the "thinly veiled contempt" with which Hayne
   detected Southern writers were treated. Brooks recounts
   his lack of acceptance by Charleston writers and his envy
   of the Boston writers' circle.

3 DAVIS, RICHARD B. "An Unpublished Poem by Paul Hamilton
   Hayne." <u>American Literature</u>, XVIII (January), 327-329.
        This untitled manuscript shows Hayne's decisions on
   changed words in revision.

4 _____. "Paul Hamilton Hayne's Debt to Dr. Francis Peyre
   Porcher." <u>Studies in Philology</u>, XLIV (July), 529-548.
        These letters from 1864-1872 reveal Hayne's critical
   views and poetic labors. Dr. Porcher had helped to form
   "the Saturday Night Club" which included Simms and Timrod.

5 GRIFFIN, MAX L. "Whittier and Hayne: A Record of Friendship."
   <u>American Literature</u>, XIX (March), 41-58.
        Indicates that the friends met in 1873 and 1879, though
   they had begun corresponding in 1853. They were eager to
   destroy sectional prejudices so Hayne praised Whittier as
   Wordsworth's equal, and Whittier admired Timrod greatly.
   Although Whittier failed to get Hayne's later poems published, he did anthologize two.

6 PAINE, GREGORY. <u>Southern Prose Writers</u>. New York: American
   Book Company, pp. lxxxii-lxxxv.
        Sees the excellence of <u>Russell's Magazine</u> as resulting
   from Hayne's editorship.

7 SIEGLER, MILLEDGE S. "Henry Timrod and Sophie Sosnowski."
   <u>Georgia Historical Quarterly</u>, XXXI (September), 171-180.
        Hayne knew Timrod during Timrod's love affair and cor-
   responded with him.

1948 A BOOKS - NONE

1948 B SHORTER WRITINGS

1 LANG, CECIL. "Swinburne and American Literature: With Six
   Hitherto Unpublished Letters." <u>American Literature</u>, XIX
   (January), 336-350.
        Swinburne "heeded only Paul Hamilton Hayne" among South-
   ern poets, for his verses gave "a charming idea of the song
   they so lovingly describe."

2   McKEITHAN, DANIEL M.   "Paul Hamilton Hayne Writes to the
      Granddaughter of Patrick Henry." Georgia Historical
      Quarterly, XXXII (March), 22-28.
          In these letters of 1854 and 1859, Hayne comments on the
      poor sale of books in Charleston and identifies true poets
      as national, not sectional.

1949 A BOOKS - NONE

1949 B SHORTER WRITINGS

1   CONNER, JOHN F. Cosmic Optimism. Gainesville: University
      of Florida Press, pp. 161, 199.
          Notes Hayne's interest in pre-existence in a poem and
      his concern for life-after-death in a letter to Bayard
      Taylor.

1950 A BOOKS - NONE

1950 B SHORTER WRITINGS

1   DEDMOND, FRANCIS B.   "Paul Hamilton Hayne and the Poe
      Westminster Memorial." Maryland Historical Magazine, XLV
      (June), 149-151.
          Though few ever knew it, Hayne was instrumental in
      memorializing Poe.

1951 A BOOKS

1   BECKER, KATE H. Paul Hamilton Hayne: Life and Letters.
      Belmont, North Carolina: The Outline Company, 145pp.
          Describes Hayne's work purely in terms of his life.

1951 B SHORTER WRITINGS

1   DAVIS, RICHARD B.   "An Uncollected Elegy by Paul Hamilton
      Hayne." South Carolina Historical and Genealogical
      Magazine, LII (January), 52-54.
          Suggests that this elegy to a Mexican War colonel was
      printed in a local paper.

2   _____.   "The Southern Dilemma: Two Unpublished Letters of
      Paul Hamilton Hayne." Journal of Southern History, XVII
      (February), 64-70.

1951

>   These letters concern Boston literary life and general
> personal matters.

3   DEDMOND, FRANCIS B. "The Poems of Paul Hamilton Hayne to
>   Frances Christine Fisher." North Carolina Historical
>   Review, XXVIII (October), 408–413.
>   Hayne sent Frances Fisher several poems for criticism
>   and flattered her as the subject of two.

4   DUFFY, CHARLES. "A Southern Genteelist: Letters of Paul
>   Hamilton Hayne to Julia C. R. Dorr." South Carolina
>   Historical and Genealogical Magazine, LII (April), 65–73.
>   In these eighteen letters written between 1878–1885,
>   Hayne praises Dorr's verse as "sincere though it lacks dis-
>   crimination" and boasts of his contacts with important
>   literary men. Duffy suggests Hayne "affected a shabby
>   genteelism imitative of Longfellow."

5   ____. "A Southern Genteelist: Letters by Paul Hamilton
>   Hayne to Julia C. R. Dorr." South Carolina Historical and
>   Genealogical Magazine, LII (July), 154–165.
>   Hayne belabors Whitman as a "Yahoo" who undermines the
>   very conception of what a poet is.

6   ____. "A Southern Genteelist: Letters by Paul Hamilton
>   Hayne to Julia C. R. Dorr." South Carolina Historical and
>   Genealogical Magazine, LII (October), 207–217.
>   Apropos of her sonnets on Sidney Lanier's death, Hayne
>   praises Dorr warmly. Rejects Emerson's "Vague species of
>   half-Pantheistic philosophy."

7   GOHDES, CLARENCE. A Literary History of the American People.
>   Edited by Arthur H. Quinn. New York: Appleton, Century,
>   Crofts, passim.
>   Feels Hayne failed at narrative.

1952 A BOOKS - NONE

1952 B SHORTER WRITINGS

1   BEATTY, RICHARD; FLOYD WATKINS; THOMAS YOUNG; and THOMAS
>   RANDALL, eds. The Literature of the South. New York:
>   Scott, Foresman, pp. 332–340.
>   Assert that Hayne's Legends and Lyrics is his best volume
>   of poems and that "he wrote too much and revised his first
>   drafts too infrequently."

2   DUFFY, CHARLES. "A Southern Genteelist: Letters of Paul
     Hamilton Hayne to Julia C. R. Dorr." <u>South Carolina
     Historical and Genealogical Magazine</u>, LIII (January), 19–30.
        Worrying about his failing reputation, Hayne attacks
    George W. Cable and insists he betrayed the South.

3   HARWELL, R. B. "A Confederate View of the Southern Poets."
     <u>American Literature</u>, XXIV (March), 51–61.
        Describes the <u>Southern Illustrated News</u> and reprints
    Hayne's "The Southern Lyric" which appeared in its July 4,
    1863, issue.

4   ROUSE, H. BLAIR and FLOYD WATKINS. "Some Manuscript Poems by
     Paul Hamilton Hayne." <u>Emory University Quarterly</u>, VIII
     (June), 83–91.
        Describe several poems of 1883 on pages of an anthro-
    pology book. Despite many revisions, only three of the
    poems are complete. One chides Mrs. "Stonewall" Jackson
    for her friendship with General Butler. Another poem
    praises the St. Louis Exposition and the third, "The Last
    Patch," concerns Reconstruction.

1953 A BOOKS – NONE

1953 B SHORTER WRITINGS

1   DEDMOND, FRANCIS B. "Paul Hamilton Hayne's 'Poe': A Note on
     a Poem." <u>Georgia Historical Quarterly</u>, XXXVII (March),
     52–53.
        Sees Hayne's "deep admiration" for Poe in this poem,
    part of the memorial edition with Millet's etchings and
    Mallarmé's famous tribute.

2   SPILLER, ROBERT, et al. <u>Literary History of the United States</u>.
     New York: Macmillan, pp. 318–320.
        Asserts that Hayne's edition of Timrod was his most im-
    portant contribution to literature, since Hayne had been
    endowed with everything more generously than Timrod--except
    poetic inspiration.

1954 A BOOKS – NONE

1954 B SHORTER WRITINGS

1   HUBBELL, JAY B. <u>The South in American Literature, 1607–1900</u>.
     Durham, North Carolina: Duke University Press, pp. 743–757,
    773–777, 935–937.

1955

> In these notes to Hayne's work, Hubbell asserts that
> Hayne was "an important literary link between the Old South
> and the New." But he was a "belated Romanticist" and senti-
> mentalist, and neither a reformer, a man of ideas, nor a
> serious nature poet. Thus, Hayne was simply "unadaptable"
> for the New South. Perhaps for these reasons the relation-
> ship of Hayne to Lanier was both cordial and strained.

1955 A BOOKS - NONE

1955 B SHORTER WRITINGS

1 CANTRELL, CLYDE and WALTON PATRICK. Southern Literary Culture.
   Birmingham: University of Alabama Press, passim.
   Lists about two dozen theses concerning Hayne.

2 DEDMOND, FRANCIS B. "Editor Hayne to Editor Kingsbury: Three
   Significant Unpublished Letters." North Carolina
   Historical Review, XXXII (January), 92-101.
   These 1858-1859 letters discuss Southern literary and
   journalistic matters.

3 PARKS, EDD WINFIELD. "Hayne's Adaptation of Chaucer's
   Franklin's Tale," in Essays in Honor of Walter Clyde Curry.
   Edited by a committee. Nashville, Tennessee: Vanderbilt
   University Press, pp. 103-115.
   Shows that Hayne's "Wife of Brittany" was not an original
   poem, as Hayne thought, but it was not a slavish imitation
   of Chaucer either. Having little interest in Chaucer's
   courtly love versus marital responsibility theme, Hayne emphasized unity of action, character consistency, coherence
   in narrative voice, and less mystery. He "whitened" the
   wife and squire, and he deleted the Franklin and his "Pro-
   logue." At first very enthusiastic, Lanier later had second
   thoughts.

1957 A BOOKS - NONE

1957 B SHORTER WRITINGS

1 PARKS, EDD WINFIELD. "When Paul Hamilton Hayne Fought a Duel."
   Georgia Review, XI (Spring), 80-84.
   Parks thinks that this duel shows that Hayne "had far
   more emotional tension, far more proneness to over-powering
   anger, than most of us have thought--and with these, far
   more self-control."

2   ____. "Paul Hamilton Hayne Eclectic Critic of Poetry."
Mississippi Quarterly, X (Fall), 155–176.
Methodically examines the literary recognition Hayne en-
countered as editor and reviewer of poetry and fiction. He
judged literary works by taste and morality, rather than
aesthetic standards, and was most tolerant of the efforts
of his friends. Thus, he overpraises Simms and disparages
James. Revised in 1962.B2.

1958 A BOOKS - NONE

1958 B SHORTER WRITINGS

1 COHEN, HENIG. "John Esten Cooke to Paul Hamilton Hayne, 1873."
South Carolina Historical Magazine, LIX (July), 139–142.
Cooke urges Hayne to write the life of Simms.

2 GREEN, CLAUDE B. "Charles Colcock Jones, Jr. and Paul Hamilton
Hayne," in Georgians in Profile. Edited by Horace
Montgomery. Athens: University of Georgia Press,
pp. 245–260.
Charles Jones, mayor of Savannah in 1860, became Hayne's
friend in 1877. Hayne relied on Jones' financial advice.
Since Jones, like Hayne, despised Whitman and rejected
Naturalism, Hayne asked him to read his "Battle of King's
Mountain" publicly in 1880 when Hayne was ill.

3 PARKS, EDD WINFIELD. "Paul Hamilton Hayne on Novels and
Novelists." Georgia Review, XII (Fall), 305–315.
Explains that Hayne chiefly admired George Eliot, Walter
Scott, Charles Dickens, and Nathaniel Hawthorne, regretting
that he found Simms' books "too carelessly written." Since
Hayne preferred romance to realism, he rejected Cable,
Howells, and Henry James at sight.

1960 A BOOKS - NONE

1960 B SHORTER WRITINGS

1 JONES, JOSEPH, et al. "Paul Hamilton Hayne," in their American
Literary Manuscripts. Austin: University of Texas Press,
pp. 165–166.
Lists various libraries where Hayne manuscripts may be
found.

1961

1961 A BOOKS - NONE

1961 B SHORTER WRITINGS

1   SMITH, HERBERT F. "Some Unpublished Letters of Paul Hamilton
     Hayne." Journal of the Rutgers University Library, XXV
     (December), 24-27.
          Reviews Hayne's correspondence with Charles Deshler
     1885-1886. Since Deshler had published a review of Hayne's
     work in Harper's (1885.B1), Hayne sought Deshler's help in
     publishing more work in that magazine. These last letters
     frankly picture the hardships of Reconstruction on Hayne's
     family.

1962 A BOOKS - NONE

1962 B SHORTER WRITINGS

1   FLORY, CLAUDE R. "Paul Hamilton Hayne and the New South."
     Georgia Historical Quarterly, XLVI (December), 388-394.
          Indicates that although Hayne disagreed with Lanier about
     the rise of the New South, he foresaw the importance of cot-
     ton to the future of the South and expressed this in his
     "Return of Peace," an ode which envisioned the New South as
     "purveyor of divinest clarity."

2   PARKS, EDD W. Ante-Bellum Southern Literary Critics. Athens:
     University of Georgia Press, pp. 227-259, 329-344.
          Revision of 1957.B2. Ten additional pages have been
     added, examining Hayne as a critic of contemporary litera-
     ture.

3   WILSON, EDMUND. Patriotic Gore. New York: Oxford University
     Press, passim.
          Notes Hayne's resistance to the realism of Cable.

1963 A BOOKS - NONE

1963 B SHORTER WRITINGS

1   BLANC, JACOB. "Paul Hamilton Hayne," in his Bibliography of
     American Literature. Vol. IV. New Haven, Connecticut:
     Yale University Press, pp. 64-74.
          Provides an authoritative listing of all editions of
     Hayne's work and correspondence. Also includes some re-
     printings of his work.

1964 A BOOKS - NONE

1964 B SHORTER WRITINGS

1   CARTER, J. A. "Paul Hamilton Hayne's Sonnet 'To the New
    South.'" Georgia Historical Quarterly, XLVIII (June),
    192-196.
        Written about 1881, this poem praises the New South
    while respecting the Old South.

2   PARKS, EDD W. Henry Timrod. New York: Twayne United States
    Authors Series, no. 53, passim.
        Examines Hayne's essay on Timrod and the mutual promo-
    tion which Timrod and Hayne gave to one another as editors
    of various ante-bellum publications.

1965 A BOOKS - NONE

1965 B SHORTER WRITINGS

1   ATCHISON, RAY M. "Scott's Monthly Magazine: A Georgia
    Post-Bellum Periodical of Literature and Military History."
    Georgia Historical Quarterly, XLIX (September), 294-305.
        Notes that Hayne was a regular contributor to Scott's
    ("one of the most important Southern magazines devoted to
    the Lost Cause") after 1869.

2   HART, JAMES. "Paul Hamilton Hayne," in The Oxford Companion
    to American Literature. Edited by the author. New York:
    Oxford University Press, p. 359.
        Sketches Hayne's life, calling his poetry "fragile,
    charming."

3   WILLIAMS, JOHN. "Hayne's 'The Prostrate South to the Radical
    North.'" Georgia Historical Quarterly, XLIX (March),
    98-101.
        This inflamatory Reconstruction poem, withheld by Hayne
    from his 1882 Complete Poems, may have been inspired by
    Father Ryan.

1966 A BOOKS - NONE

1966 B SHORTER WRITINGS

1   NOLTE, EUGENE. "Two Unpublished Letters from Paul Hamilton
    Hayne." Georgia Historical Quarterly, L (March), 105-109.

1966

           Hayne protests Northern policies toward the South in one letter, and in the other he thanks Mrs. Toland for her book of poems.

2   WALSER, RICHARD. "Seven 'Lost' Sonnets of Paul Hamilton Hayne." <u>Bulletin of the New York Public Library</u>, LXX (October), 533–537.
        Reproduces seven sonnets, 1865–1867, published in <u>Southern Field and Fireside</u>.

<u>1967 A BOOKS – NONE</u>

<u>1967 B SHORTER WRITINGS</u>

1   OWENS, GUY. <u>The Thirties: Fiction, Poetry, Drama</u>. Deland, Florida: Everett/Edwards, pp. 159–167.
        Notes that by the 1930's the "shades of Timrod, Lanier, and Hayne were exorcised."

2   WAGENKNECHT, EDWARD. <u>John Greenleaf Whittier: Portrait in Paradox</u>. New York: Oxford University Press, passim.
        Indicates that Hayne's heart "rejoiced" in Whittier's praise of Henry Timrod.

<u>1968 A BOOKS – NONE</u>

<u>1968 B SHORTER WRITINGS</u>

1   EATON, CLEMENT. <u>The Waning of the Old South Civilization, 1860–1880's</u>. Athens: University of Georgia Press, pp. 98–99.
        Summarizes Hayne's involvement in the war as man and poet.

2   IFKOVIC, EDWARD. "Two Poems for Paul Hamilton Hayne." <u>American Notes and Queries</u>, VI (January), 71–72.
        Suggests that these poems by Catharine G. Poyas show that she borrowed sea images and the poet-prophet idea from Hayne.

3   MOORE, RAYBURN S. "Paul Hamilton Hayne." <u>Georgia Review</u>, XXII (Spring), 106–124.
        Moore provides a biographical survey of Hayne's life and asserts that Hayne devoted himself more completely to the literary life than either Poe or Simms. Reprinted in 1972.A1.

1969 A BOOKS - NONE

1969 B SHORTER WRITINGS

1   MOORE, RAYBURN S.   "Hayne the Poet: A New Look."   South
     Carolina Review, II (November), 4-13.
          Asserts that although Hayne is a weak poet, the range
     and output of his verse make him worthy of examination once
     again.

2   _____. "Paul Hamilton Hayne," in A Bibliographical Guide to
     the Study of Southern Literature. Edited by Louis D. Rubin,
     Jr. Baton Rouge: University of Louisiana Press,
     pp. 215-217.
          Provides a summary of the state of Hayne bibliography
     and a highly selective list of secondary items.

1970 A BOOKS - NONE

1970 B SHORTER WRITINGS

1   SIMMS, L. MOODY, JR.   "Paul Hamilton Hayne's Method of Poetic
     Composition." Mississippi Quarterly, XXIV (Winter), 57-62.
          An edition of the essay by William Hamilton Hayne, "Paul
     Hamilton Hayne's Methods of Poetic Composition." Identical
     to the previous printing 1892.B1, Simms reprinted it be-
     cause it was never collected.

1971 A BOOKS - NONE

1971 B SHORTER WRITINGS

1   ANON. "Paul Hamilton Hayne." Encyclopaedia Britannica.
     Vol. XI. Chicago: William Benton, p. 198.
          This biographical sketch emphasizes Hayne's pre-Civil
     War experiences.

2   RAÏZIS, M. BYRON. "Paul Hamilton Hayne [He physe stin
     romantiki poiisi---hena paradeigma]." Epeirotike Hestia,
     XX:109-110.

1972 A BOOKS

1   MOORE, RAYBURN S. Paul Hamilton Hayne. Twayne United States
     Authors Series, no. 202. New York: Twayne, 193pp.

1972

Provides a Preface, Chronology, and seven chapters including a "Biographical Sketch," "Early Poetry, 1845-65,"
"Legends and Lyrics, 1872," and other chapters on Hayne's
books of verse. Feels that Hayne has been under-rated since
he wrote "completely contrived verse." In the English poetic mainstream, he was indebted to Morris and Tennyson.
This has obscured his own qualities, which are most closely
related to Keats and Hunt. He was at his best as a son-
neteer. See 1968.B3.

1972 B SHORTER WRITINGS

1   HUBBELL, JAY B. Who Are the Major American Writers? Durham,
     North Carolina: Duke University Press, pp. 38, 116.
         In this protracted reputation study, Hubbell notes that
     Edwin Whipple, influential New England critic, thought
     highly of Hayne in 1876. Elsewhere he recounts Hayne's bit-
     terness with W. D. Howells who gave the impression, as At-
     lantic editor, of wanting only poems "of the Wordsworthian
     stamp."

2   MOORE, RAYBURN S. "The Old South and the New: Paul Hamilton
     Hayne and Maurice Thompson." Southern Literary Journal, V
     (Fall), 108-122.
         Suggests that the Hayne-Thompson relationship reveals
     the influence of post-bellum politics upon the friendship
     and the literary views of these two minor writers. Their
     letters show that they differed mainly over their inter-
     pretation of the post-bellum South.

1973 A BOOKS - NONE

1973 B SHORTER WRITINGS

1   MOORE, RAYBURN S. "Paul Hamilton Hayne and Northern
     Magazines, 1866-1886," in Essays Mostly on Periodical
     Publishing in America: A Collection in Honor of Clarence
     Gohdes. Edited by James Woodress. Durham, North Carolina:
     Duke University Press, pp. 134-147.
         By 1870 Hayne had contributed to several Northern maga-
     zines, most notably the monthlies (Lippincott's, Scribner's-
     Century, Harper's and Atlantic). At first cordially recep-
     tive, their later rejections caused Hayne to feel most
     Northern magazines were "closed" to him and biased against
     the South. Some of Hayne's best poems were published in
     these journals--an "Ode" to Bryant which he appreciated,

and "Snow Messengers" a tribute to Whittier and Longfellow
which they liked.

2   SMITH, SIMON M., JR.   Review of Moore's <u>Paul Hamilton Hayne</u>.
     <u>South Carolina Historical Magazine</u>, LXXIV (January), 44.
         The book is restrained in its praise, though "sound."
     <u>See</u> 1972.A1.

3   YOUNG, THOMAS DANIEL.   "How Time Has Served Two Southern Poets:
     Paul Hamilton Hayne and Sidney Lanier."   <u>Southern Literary
     Journal</u>, VI (Fall), 101-110.
         Finds Moore's attempt to place Hayne as a minor poet in
     a complex milieu is rather successful. <u>See</u> 1972.A1.

<u>1974 A BOOKS - NONE</u>

<u>1974 B SHORTER WRITINGS</u>

1   STAUFFER, DONALD BARLOW.   <u>A Short History of American Poetry</u>.
     New York: E. P. Dutton, pp. 189-190.
         Asserts that Hayne typified the Southern writer's predi-
     cament before the Civil War--the quest for wider audiences.
     Hence, Hayne went North to publish at the prestigious Boston
     presses, but the writers he met in Boston aggravated his
     dissatisfaction with the South.   Stauffer contends that
     even had Hayne lived in the North he would not have been a
     better poet.   His poems "virtually ignore the real world."

2   THOMPSON, G. R.   Review of Moore's <u>Paul Hamilton Hayne</u>, in
     <u>American Literary Scholarship, An Annual/1972</u>.   Edited by
     J. Albert Robbins.   Durham, North Carolina: Duke
     University Press, pp. 232-233.
         Contends that Moore's "informed and critically astute
     assessment" makes persuasive his elevation of the poet over
     other Southern versifiers. <u>See</u> 1972.A1.

Indexes

Index — Sidney Lanier

"Possibilities of the South in
     Literature, The," 1898.B7
Pratt, Waldo, 1929.B6; 1930.B5
Prejudices, Third Series,
     1922.B3
Preminger, Alex, 1965.B7
"Present Relationship of Prose
     to Verse, The," 1953.B4
Prophetic Tradition in American
     Poetry, 1835-1900, 1968.B5
Prosody, 1903.B9; 1904.B4, B8;
     1907.B2, B6; 1911.B2;
     1921.B4; 1935.B1; 1941.A2;
     1945.B3; 1948.B6-B7; 1972.A1
"Psalm of the West, The,"
     1885.B7; 1933.A1, B14;
     1962.B1; 1973.B4; 1975.B1

Questions at Issue, 1893.B2
Quinn, Arthur, 1951.B2

Ransom, John Crowe, 1934.B3;
     1940.B9-B11; 1961.B1;
     1976.B2
"Raven Days," 1965.B2
"Reading Interests of Thoreau,
     Hawthorne and Lanier, The,"
     1969.B9
"Realism in Sidney Lanier's
     Tiger-Lilies," 1971.B3
Reality and Myth: Essays in
     American Literature in
     Memory of Richard Croom
     Beatty, 1964.B3
Reamer, Owen, 1969.B8
"Recent Movement in Southern
     Literature, The," 1887.B1
"Recollections of a Naval
     Life," 1900.B3
Rede, Kenneth, 1926.B6; 1933.B9
Redmond, James, 1973.B6
Rees, Robert, 1971.B2
Reese, Lizette, 1926.B1
"Remembering the Beauty,"
     1940.A1
Reminiscences and Sketches,
     1908.B12
Reminiscences of Famous
     Georgians, 1908.B4-B5
"Reminiscences of Sidney Lanier,"
     (Allen), 1895.B1

"Reminiscences of Sidney Lanier,"
     (Clifford Lanier), 1895.B7
"Reminiscences of Sidney Lanier,"
     (White), 1929.B11
Representative Authors of
     Maryland, 1911.B4
Representative Southern Poets,
     1906.B9
Retrospects and Prospects,
     1899.B3-B4, B12; 1945.B6;
     1972.A1
"Revenge of Hamish, The,"
     1931.B2; 1936.B10; 1962.B4
Rhythm of Beowulf, The, 1942.B3
Ribbens, Dennis, 1969.B9
Richardson, Charles, 1888.B9
Richter, Jean-Paul, 1945.B6;
     1968.B2; 1972.A1
"Rise of Realism, 1871-1891,
     The," (Robert P. Falk),
     1953.B3
Rise of Realism, The, 1953.B3
Roadside Meetings, 1930.B1
"Roadside Meetings of a Literary
     Nomad," 1929.B2
Road to Reunion, The, 1937.B1
Romanticism and Nationalism in
     the Old South, 1949.B4
Roots of Southern Writing, The,
     1972.B3
Roquie, Margaret, 1937.B3
Rosebery, Marguerite, 1944.B3
Ross, Robert, 1961.B2
Rossetti, Dante G., 1893.B3
Routh, James E., Jr., 1910.B2
Rovit, Earl, 1960.B6
Royce, Josiah, 1892.B3
Rubin, Louis D., Jr., 1969.B7,
     B10; 1975.B1; 1976.B2
Russell, Charles, 1929.B7
Rutherford, Mildred, 1894.B4;
     1906.B10-B11
Ryan, Carson, 1939.B7

Saintsbury, G. E. B., 1910.B3
"Samuel Knox--a Patriot," 1924.B3
Sapir, Edward, 1921.B4
Scherer, James A., 1906.B12
Scholes, Percy, 1955.B2
Scholl, Evelyn, 1948.B6

Index — Henry Timrod

Index — Paul Hamilton Hayne